Extinction Events and Dawn Chorus

33 1/3 Global

33 1/3 Global, a series related to but independent from **33 1/3**, takes the format of the original series of short, music-based books and brings the focus to music throughout the world. With initial volumes focusing on Japanese and Brazilian music, the series will also include volumes on the popular music of Australia/Oceania, Europe, Africa, the Middle East, and more.

33 1/3 Japan

Series Editor: Noriko Manabe

Spanning a range of artists and genres—from the 1970s rock of Happy End to technopop band Yellow Magic Orchestra, the Shibuya-kei of Cornelius, classic anime series *Cowboy Bebop*, J-Pop/EDM hybrid Perfume, and vocaloid star Hatsune Miku—33 1/3 Japan is a series devoted to in-depth examination of Japanese popular music of the twentieth and twenty-first centuries.

Published Titles:

Supercell's *Supercell* by Keisuke Yamada
AKB48 by Patrick W. Galbraith and Jason G. Karlin
Yoko Kanno's *Cowboy Bebop Soundtrack* by Rose Bridges
Perfume's *Game* by Patrick St. Michel
Cornelius's *Fantasma* by Martin Roberts
Joe Hisaishi's *My Neighbor Totoro: Soundtrack* by Kunio Hara
Shonen Knife's *Happy Hour* by Brooke McCorkle
Nenes' *Koza Dabasa* by Henry Johnson
Yuming's *The 14th Moon* by Lasse Lehtonen
Toshiko Akiyoshi-Lew Tabackin Big Band's *Kogun* by E. Taylor Atkins
S.O.B.'s *Don't Be Swindle* by Mahon Murphy and Ran Zwigenberg

Forthcoming Titles:

Kohaku Utagassen: The Red and White Song Contest by Shelley Brunt

Yellow Magic Orchestra's *Yellow Magic Orchestra* by Toshiyuki Ohwada

33 1/3 Brazil

Series Editor: Jason Stanyek

Covering the genres of samba, tropicália, rock, hip hop, forró, bossa nova, heavy metal and funk, among others, 33 1/3 Brazil is a series devoted to in-depth examination of the most important Brazilian albums of the twentieth and twenty-first centuries.

Published Titles:

Caetano Veloso's *A Foreign Sound* by Barbara Browning

Tim Maia's *Tim Maia Racional Vols. 1 &2* by Allen Thayer

João Gilberto and Stan Getz's *Getz/Gilberto* by Brian McCann

Gilberto Gil's *Refazenda* by Marc A. Hertzman

Dona Ivone Lara's *Sorriso Negro* by Mila Burns

Milton Nascimento and Lô Borges's *The Corner Club* by Jonathon Grasse

Racionais MCs' *Sobrevivendo no Inferno* by Derek Pardue

Naná Vasconcelos's *Saudades* by Daniel B. Sharp

Chico Buarque's First *Chico Buarque* by Charles A. Perrone

Forthcoming Titles:

Jorge Ben Jor's *África Brasil* by Frederick J. Moehn

33 1/3 Europe

Series Editor: Fabian Holt

Spanning a range of artists and genres, 33 1/3 Europe offers engaging accounts of popular and culturally significant albums of Continental Europe and the North Atlantic from the twentieth and twenty-first centuries.

Published Titles:

Darkthrone's *A Blaze in the Northern Sky* by Ross Hagen

Ivo Papazov's *Balkanology* by Carol Silverman

Heiner Müller and Heiner Goebbels's *Wolokolamsker Chaussee* by Philip V. Bohlman

Modeselektor's *Happy Birthday!* by Sean Nye

Mercyful Fate's *Don't Break the Oath* by Henrik Marstal

Bea Playa's *I'll Be Your Plaything* by Anna Szemere and András Rónai

Various Artists' *DJs do Guetto* by Richard Elliott

Czesław Niemen's *Niemen Enigmatic* by Ewa Mazierska and Mariusz Gradowski

Massada's *Astaganaga* by Lutgard Mutsaers

Los Rodriguez's *Sin Documentos* by Fernán del Val and Héctor Fouce

Édith Piaf's *Récital 1961* by David Looseley

Nuovo Canzoniere Italiano's *Bella Ciao* by Jacopo Tomatis

Iannis Xenakis's *Persepolis* by Aram Yardumian

Vopli Vidopliassova's *Tantsi* by Maria Sonevytsky

Amália Rodrigues's *Amália at the Olympia* by Lila Ellen Gray

Ardit Gjebrea's *Projekt Jon* by Nicholas Tochka

Aqua's *Aquarium* by C.C. McKee

J.M.K.E.'s *To the Cold Land* by Brigitta Davidjants

Taco Hemingway's *Jarmark* by Kamila Rymajdo

Einstürzende Neubauten's *Kollaps* by Melle Jan Kromhout and Jan Nieuwenhuis

CCCP—FEDELI ALLA LINEA's *Affinità—Divergenze Fra il Compagno Togliatti e Noi* by Giacomo Bottà

Silly's *Februar* by Michael Rauhut

Forthcoming Titles:

Sigur Rós' *Ágætis Byrjun* by Tore Størvold

Aphrodite's Child's *666* by Ana Leorne

33 1/3 Oceania

Series Editors: Jon Stratton (senior editor) and Jon Dale (specializing in books on albums from Aotearoa/New Zealand)

Spanning a range of artists and genres from Australian Indigenous artists to Maori and Pasifika artists, from Aotearoa/New Zealand noise music to Australian rock, and including music from Papua and other Pacific islands, 33 1/3 Oceania offers exciting accounts of albums that illustrate the wide range of music made in the Oceania region.

Published Titles:

John Farnham's *Whispering Jack* by Graeme Turner
The Church's *Starfish* by Chris Gibson
Regurgitator's *Unit* by Lachlan Goold and Lauren Istvandity
Kylie Minogue's *Kylie* by Adrian Renzo and Liz Giuffre
Alastair Riddell's *Space Waltz* by Ian Chapman
Hunters & Collectors's *Human Frailty* by Jon Stratton
The Front Lawn's *Songs from the Front Lawn* by Matthew Bannister
Bic Runga's *Drive* by Henry Johnson
The Dead C's *Clyma est mort* by Darren Jorgensen
Ed Kuepper's *Honey Steel's Gold* by John Encarnacao
Chain's *Toward the Blues* by Peter Beilharz
Hilltop Hoods' *The Calling* by Dianne Rodger
Screamfeeder's *Kitten Licks* by Ben Green and Ian Rogers
The Clean's *Boodle Boodle Boodle* by Geoff Stahl
The Avalanches' *Since I Left You* by Charles Fairchild
John Sangster's *Lord of the Rings Vols. 1-3* by Bruce Johnson
Soundtrack from *Saturday Night Fever* by Clinton Walker
Eyeliner's *BUY NOW* by Michael Brown
TISM's *Machiavelli and the Four Seasons* by Tyler Jenke

Crowded House's *Together Alone* by Barnaby Smith
Silverchair's *Frogstomp* by Jay Daniel Thompson
Various Artists' *Truckload of Sky: The Lost Songs of David McComb* by Glenn D'Cruz
Robert Forster's *Danger in the Past* by Patrick Chapman
Tame Impala's *Currents* by Alister Newstead
The La De Da's *The Happy Prince* by John Tebbutt
The Three Out's *Move* by James Gaunt
Dick Diver's *Calendar Days* by Mitch Ryan
Gary Shearston's *Dingo* by Peter Mills
Liza Lim's *Extinction Events and Dawn Chorus* by Ty Bouque

Forthcoming Titles:

The Triffids' *Born Sandy Devotional* by Christina Ballico
5MMM's *Compilation Album of Adelaide Bands 1980* by Collette Snowden
INXS' *Kick* by Lauren Moxey
Sunnyboys' *Sunnyboys* by Stephen Bruel
Kate Ceberano's *Brave* by Panizza Allmark
Dinah Lee's *Introducing Dinah Lee* by Kimberly Cannady
The Waifs' *Up All Night* by Rebecca Bennison
Split Enz' *Mental Notes* by Michael Lamb
Douglas Lilburn's *Complete Electro-Acoustic Works* by Bruce Russell
Savage Garden's *Affirmation* by Pat O'Grady
Blood Duster's *Fisting the Dead* by Rosemary Overell
Olivia Newton-John's *Physical* by Jarrod Sturnieks
Stella Donnelly's *Beware of the Dogs* by Emily Wilson

33 1/3 South Asia

Series Editor: Natalie Sarrazin

From the films of Bollywood and Lollywood, to home-grown *bhangra* hip-hop, Hindu devotional pop and Sufi rock, Sri Lankan rap, Indo jazz and disco, new-wave electronica and diasporic Asian Underground scene, 33 1/3 South Asia takes readers on a sonically diverse journey through the most significant soundtracks and albums from the twentieth and twenty-first centuries.

Published Titles:

Dil Chahta Hai Soundtrack by Jayson Beaster-Jones

Lata Mangeshkar's *My Favourites, Volume 2* by Anirudha Bhattacharjee and Chandrashekhar Rao

Coke Studio (Season 14) by Rakae Rehman Jamil and Khadija Muzaffar

33 1/3 Africa

Series Editor: Michael Veal

33 1/3 Africa is a series of books on canonical, album-length works of African music, including traditional music, experimental music, and, with particular emphasis, popular music. Academic and journalistic writing results in sophisticated, nuanced, and accessible narratives on African music.

Published Titles:

Fela Anikulapo-Kuti's *Sorrow Tears and Blood* by Stephanie Shonekan

Forthcoming Titles:

Cesária Évora's *Miss Perfumado* by Jacqueline Georgis

Paul Simon's *Graceland* by Kalvin Schmidt-Rimpler Dinh

Nico, Rochereau, Roger & L'African Fiesta—*Volume 1 (1962–1963)* by Frank Gunderson

Extinction Events and Dawn Chorus

Ty Bouque

33 1/3 OCEANIA

Series Editor: Jon Stratton,
UniSA Creative, University of South Australia, and
Jon Dale, University of Melbourne, Australia

BLOOMSBURY ACADEMIC
NEW YORK • LONDON • OXFORD • NEW DELHI • SYDNEY

BLOOMSBURY ACADEMIC
Bloomsbury Publishing Inc, 1359 Broadway, New York, NY 10018, USA
Bloomsbury Publishing Plc, 50 Bedford Square, London, WC1B 3DP, UK
Bloomsbury Publishing Ireland, 29 Earlsfort Terrace, Dublin 2, D02 AY28, Ireland

First published in the United States of America 2026

Library of Congress Control Number: 2026942164

ISBN: HB: 979-8-216-44314-8
PB: 979-8-216-44313-1
ePDF: 979-8-216-44316-2
eBook: 979-8-216-44315-5

Series: 33 1/3 Oceania

Typeset by Integra Software Services Pvt. Ltd.
Printed and bound in the United States of America

For product safety-related questions contact productsafety@bloomsbury.com.

To find out more about our authors and books visit www.bloomsbury.com and sign up for our newsletters.

Contents

Acknowledgments

My thanks to Jon Stratton, Rachel Moore, Alex Sobrino, and the diligent team at Bloomsbury, without whose extravagant patience, assurances, and stewardship this book would have seen nary a dawn, much less its own. Many thanks, too, go to the friends, advisors, colleagues, and anonymous readers whose thoughtful suggestions and careful re-readings of various drafts improved this book tenfold. Teresa Turnage deserves a special mention for heroic efforts. All remaining errors are my own. Thanks go to Liza, for her generosity, her nudgings, and her humor; to Steve, for being game; to Ti, for many years in the unofficial book club; to Seth, for bringing me tête-à-tête with my Real; to Gramm, for ripostes and reposes that both sharpen and soften my thinking, always in exactly the right places; and, above all, to Tim Rutherford-Johnson, in the shadow of whose own towering work on Liza Lim I have only ever traced out smallish eddies. His monthly calls left fingerprints on every page of this book, and it is to and for him that this book was written. "Between the snobbery and the aspiration," Cavell wrote, "there is the daily field on which we do learn from anyone and everyone—sometimes, maybe most often, circulating the discreditable things we already know; but sometimes circling the better thing."[1] You have always circled the better thing.

Introduction: On Believing Otherwise

It is a question of what you believe an album can *do*. If you believe, as Liza Lim believes, that transmission always ferries a measure of magic. If you believe, as Liza Lim believes, that art *thinks* just as much as can be thought. If you *believe*.

The assignment given me here was to treat as album a music not originally destined for that form, to think the word *album* in place of the word *work* without conceding any semantic ground. It is the convention of media studies—of which Susan Sontag on photography is the exemplar—to read in capture and transmission an irreparable violence done to the object: "a set of photographs that freezes moments in a life or a society contradicts their form, which is a process, a flow in time."[1] Recording, in its archival manducation, enfolds the same dialectic of loss: the very gesture that would preserve an existentially fragile music for all posterity also strips sound from its instantiated liveness, absents its spontaneous interaction with a singular acoustic, and threatens to scrub away that fallible, gorgeous *grain* by which all human-made music indexes its having-been-human-made. Not for nothing is an iteration in the recording studio called a *take*, microphones always implicitly divesting from the Real a quantity of its embodied force.

It has been my charge to resist that dialectic, to engage an *album* of *concert music* as neither loss nor gain but as simply something else entirely. The gambit is that *album* has, at this late date in media history, exceeded its barren etymology. Formerly understood as absence—*album*, neuter of the Latin *albus* for *white, whiteness*, originally a clean slate on which to write signatures or edicts; its musical appointment determined on both the visual similarity of the record's dust jacket to that old *album amicorum*, the book of companionable signatures, and the ontological similarity of its *tékhnē*, its beckoning of inscription—the modern album is now encrusted with more cultural freight than can be so easily sloughed off. (A fact to which, we might point out, this series effusively attests.)

New Music[a] has traditionally taken the anthology CD as a necessary but blessedly silent intermediary, a mostly-frictionless repository by which a displaced and transient field furnishes access to itself. (Here, in my hands, a facsimile of a major contribution to the field which in one's lifetime one is not promised to hear "proper," that is, *live*.) As a consolation prize, it offers the imprimatur of record labels and the signature of composers to confer *definitive* status on a recording, a promise of interpretive fidelity whose recuperation of live performance's potential misfires implicitly shores the album against its crisis of worth: if it's not going to be live, it's going to be *perfect*.[b]

---

a When so capitalized, "New Music" refers to the decentralized field of composers, sound artists, performers, curators, and thinkers who route their loose aesthetic heredity back to European and select American modernisms of the early twentieth century, and who continue to ask the pressing questions about sound, perception, form, history, and attention; Liza Lim belongs to such a field.

b *Extinction Events* and *Songs Found in Dream* are here mastered from live performances; only *Axis Mundi* was recorded in studio. The "live" album is meant to preserve both the energy of the audience-inflected performance, as well as—in New Music especially—save money on an otherwise expensive studio process.

But no medium is silent. Not really. And certainly not when Liza Lim is around. One of the principal tenets of Lim's music is that medial transformation—the passage of energy and sound from an idiomatic source through a foreign amplifying body—always unconceals a surfeit of expressivity inaccessible in solitude. The magic of writing music lies, by Lim's own words, "in the transformative gesture through which one says 'let this thing stand for that', 'let this generate a reverberation over there.'"[2] All these objects imagined otherwise in her world—woodblocks that sing, violins that astrologize, voices that shuttle unsated angels and spirits inside—bespeak a kind of theory of entangled presence: humans are neither the sole nor even the most populous entities capable of thought, and our dreams and imaginations interleave with the ancient and unknowable dreams and imaginations of the natural world. Objects—of which musical instruments constitute a special category—retain tethers to that invisible realm, even when their social usage has erased most of that latent magic (think of the specters of labor haunting Marx's coat[3]). All it takes, however, is a willingness to see such objects slantwise, and the invisible rushes back to perception with force: with practice (and it will be something like pedagogy that emerges from this book), a woodblock can be heard singing Goethe. Lim's project rests on the belief that an ecstatic and uncontrolled *over there* is forever lying in wait, simmering just beyond the present's ragged edge: her music's controlled destabilization of the sonic field through distortion, possession, and the suturing of time is what allows it to momentarily flicker, a double exposure, another world within our own.

And so by its very orientation to presence and body, the music of Liza Lim troubles any impulse we might harbor to efface the album format as *merely* there. She would say that her music plays with "the living thought of things"[4]—a knot of interspecies and inter-material epistemologies from which the physical album cannot be so easily discounted. When those activating forces of her music pass through yet another resonating membrane, compress and explode through one further portal of mediation, it forces an additional rupture in time and space: *here*, in this room (the room of mediated listening), is a *there*, in that room (the studio of recording), *which is itself* an invocation of one further place which sits astride both but is resolutely neither. Left stranded without the semiotic stability of a visual source, this excessively mediated listener is prone to heightened delirium: if bodies and instruments are constraining vectors for the wild energies Lim summons, those energies recuperate a measure of their wildness when returned to the realm of the invisible.

It is true, of course, that things go missing when the bodies do. Listening to *Extinction Events and Dawn Chorus* on CD, one cannot visibly witness, for example, the distracting interruption of an enormous sheet of transparent crinkly cellophane as it crawls onstage to ensconce the twelve musicians. Nor can one see the writing desk, replete with lamp, at which violin and snare drum negotiate the terms of their calligraphic exchange. Or catch the moment when the band lays down their instruments in favor of an array of handheld percussion taken up in the dim light of the closing chorus. These events are reduced to sonic traces, utterly bewildering without explanatory context.

But stick with the bewilderment a moment longer. If Lim's nested repetitions—patterns of music that skip and catch in gyres of hooked time—are a curious phenomenon in live performance, they become monstrous on CD, where trips and repeats sign potential interferences of a medium gone rogue.

The cellophane event, contained by its locatable sounding source in the concert hall, rears up to the status of rupture on disc: Does that static belong to the music? Or is the playback machine "speaking" of its own accord? Ventriloquism can no longer remain a preoccupation of performance: on CD, it becomes the entire apparatus of articulation.

If we continue to take as given the album as a crippled substitute for the breathing thing, we foreclose on these opportunities to think music beyond the aesthetic, to activate its political potential for imagining and believing otherwise. So long as it remains a thinly veiled simulacrum, we castrate the album of its rich objecthood and censor its entangled presences. Contra Carolyn Abbate, there is perhaps something still to be learned from a gnostic tarrying with such objects.[5] If you *believe*.

Extinction Events and Dawn Chorus—written first for the Austrian experimental ensemble Klangforum Wien and premiered in 2018 at the music festival in Witten, Germany—culminated the conceptual arrival of the Anthropocene in Liza Lim's thought, capping what is in hindsight one of the most productive periods of musical output in modern memory. Lim's four major solo projects between 2016 and 2017 were *An Elemental Thing* for solo woodblock; *The Su Song Star Map*, for solo violin; *an ocean beyond earth*, for solo 'cello; and *The Table of Knowledge*, for solo double bass. All four are major statement pieces, explicating in long form ideas that had been latent or subconscious in Lim's thinking until that period: object ventriloquism, time on the scale of hyperobjects, geographies of extended instruments, and the magic of instrument-human hybrids, respectively. Strains of all four reappear in

Extinction Events. The year 2016 also saw the premiere of Lim's *How Forests Think*, the first ensemble work to directly invoke ecology. That project, for sheng and ensemble, took its title from Eduardo Kohn's provocation to anthropology that human epistemologies fail to account for the interconnected thinking and dreaming of animals, plants, particles, and air. *How Forests Think* is a crucial foil to *Extinction Events*: if the former checks the human's vain anthropomorphism in an environment teeming with Others, the latter sketches—without pity—the consequences of failing to learn that lesson.

But the work to which *Extinction Events* is closest is Lim's fourth opera *Tree of Codes*. Premiered in Cologne in the spring of 2016, that opera peers through the holes Jonathan Safran Foer cut out of Bruno Schulz's *Street of Crocodiles*, bearing witness to what Lim calls "an extra day grafted on to the continuity of life." There, perimeters distinguishing human from animal, instrument from voice, and nature from machine become exceptionally thin and porous. *Tree of Codes* is eschatology without etymon, a rehearsal of end times sheltered from the threatening lastness of *eskhatos*. History flows in leaks and jets, foaming in monstrous admixtures of timelines and traces. *Logos* suspends, favoring sensoria, impulse, and residue. The fantastic adumbrates the believed-possible, looking for chinks and holes.

Time and again in Lim's work, music functions as an activating trigger for a chronometric register we might call the *speculative graft*. Here, in this time outside of time, music becomes free of the perspectival chains that link it to teleology, free to take up relations that would be otherwise irreconcilable. It is in such a graft that *Extinction Events* takes place. Like the opera, the music of *Extinction Events and Dawn Chorus* carves out an imaginary duration in which to rehearse the collapse of humanity, a pocket sutured to the human timeline where extinct birds sing again, traces of Janáček swirl in ocean eddies, and string instruments catasterize by drawing maps. Its risky wager, however, is to refuse the human perspective that would experience such a collapse as tragedy. The "dawn chorus" of the title refers to the album's fifth track, an auric unfurling of sonic horizons. In 2016, it was first reported that fish off the coast of Western Australia's Port Hedland could be heard vocalizing together at sunrise. *Extinction Events* suggests that the sun will rise on the day after humanity has perished, and there will still be singing.

The speculative graft is something close to fiction, a relationship music typically permits only with extreme caution. Music is always the register to which fiction aspires; fiction, meanwhile, is a citation with which music is not wholly comfortable. Both, of course, promise access to the imaginary which is otherwise excluded from philosophy's rigorous truth and from the science's empirical verity. But music does not boast language's capacity to signify, and as an instantiated art cannot take concrete form. As a result, it gets anxious whenever asked to sustain a program: music cannot be made to assume absolute meaning.

Peggy Kamuf, however, in her *Book of Addresses*, proposes fiction's realm to be much vaster than traditionally accredited: "The question concerning fiction is not: what is it? but rather: what does it *do*?" Already we are closer to *Extinction Events*, in which what happens *to objects* carries much greater significance than *what they are*. Kamuf continues: "A fiction refers to nothing that exists. It refers, but to nothing in existence. Thus, the fiction act or operation consists in making reference but also in suspending the referent. It is a referential operation that does something with or to reference."[6] From

Kamuf's perspective, *Extinction Events and Dawn Chorus* is music-as-fiction. In its onto-historical operation, it both refers to and suspends eschatology: it casts to a place and time that does not (yet) exist and in doing so suspends any obligation to verisimilitude. In its imaginative operation, it *does something* to musical reference, raising that *something* to the subject of experience: "'let this thing stand for that'; 'let this generate a reverberation over there.'"

Attempting to account for this surfeit of relationality, this book is partitioned in to four sections, one for each of the four words that title the album's closing track. That work—*Songs found in dream*, written by Lim back in 2005—belongs to a collection of early pieces engaged with the knowledge bases of Aboriginal Australians (an engagement that presages Lim's later ecological turn). The title is derived from the Kukatja word *kalyururu*, whose adjectival meaning, "like water shimmering as it falls," describes those ephemeral strains one hears only while asleep. Taking cue from this pregnancy of a single word with entire poetic complexes, the book picks up each word as a contingent invocation to excessive close reading: or, four ways of looking at an object. Rather than explain or reduce the album to a series of facts or descriptions, it is this book's aim instead—in homage to Lim's own theory of entangled presence—to trace around the many holes, abysses, and aporias to thought that the album keeps open, with no intention of suturing them back up.

Though Liza Lim is not a Marxist by trade, one of the central theses of this book is that *Extinction Events* affirms Fredric Jameson's persistent reminder that "the pedagogical function of a work of art seems in various forms to have been an inescapable parameter of any conceivable Marxist aesthetic."[7] Art that resists capitalism—and, by extension, the ecocide it wrought—will always contain a measure of entrainment, and pedagogy by nature demands a quantity of repetition. As an aesthetic principle, Lim has been perennially fascinated with forms of altered repetition for the perspectival shifts they engender: by repeating material in slightly different ways, she draws attention to parameters like depth, angle, color, porosity, and light. The listener is "taught" to shift their ear from notes and rhythms to other, peripheral effects. It is the wager of this book that the album format, with the fantastical permission of its rewind button, provides the medial analog to *Extinction Events'* pedagogic function. That one can always go back, can listen again another way—a possibility foreclosed by the live concert—heightens the pedagogic status of *Extinction Events and Dawn Chorus*: practicing the impulse to continuous return, the album habituates us to imaginative pathways beyond the limited repertory of postmodern consciousness.

It is difficult to adequately testify to the status of the event held by this album. It struck like lightning a New Music paralyzed in its response to climate crisis, caught between fetishizing the imported liberal values of sustainability on the one hand and overstating the role of art in mitigating environmental collapse on the other. At once left-leaning, allegiant with anti-capital critique, and deeply insecure in its relationship to globalism, the paradox of New Music's aesthetic paradigm started to feel insurmountable: it is not for everyone and cannot speak as such. How, then, to say or do anything meaningful for the world?

The existential panic to validate "intellectual" creative labor in the end times caused a flurry of activity desperate to make New Music feel meaningful and prescient. As "music about climate change" became increasingly ubiquitous, the conspicuous absence of a coordinated swell of activism grew difficult to ignore. Gradually, the old Leonard Bernstein chestnut—that humanity's reply to violence will be "to make music more intensely, more beautifully, more devotedly than ever before"[8]—acquired an ironic sneer: in the age of technocracy and corporate waste, music for insider audiences, no matter how devoted in sentiment, effects no significant change. Posturing as activism and overeager to assert the legibility of a reductive referent to politics, New Music inadvertently stripped itself of the one thing it does well: architecting zones of time in which to exercise alternative modes of being, doing, and relating.

The release of *Extinction Events and Dawn Chorus* constituted a major intervention and a rare flash of hope. In its double refusal of both simple mimetic spectacle (music that "sounds like the end of humanity") and affective response (an "elegy for the human race"), Lim proposed a meaningful place in the humanitarian response to crisis that only music could fill: as an interface through which to imagine expanded and more ethical relationships to the strange timescales of ecological collapse. *Extinction Events* was a major statement from one of the field's most prominent voices that not only were the heady discourses of aesthetics not excluded from thinking with the hyperobjects of late capitalism: they were—and continue to be—the only site in which New Music could adequately claim meaningful activist status. Heralded as both a major musical achievement[c] and a significant contribution to philosophies of

[c] Both Lim's belated debut with Kairos, then one of New Music's gold-star labels, and one of *The New Yorker*'s notable albums of 2020.

the Anthropocene, *Extinction Events and Dawn Chorus* remains the standard-bearer for New Music's role in climate discourse.

One of the central provocations in Leo Bersani's *The Culture of Redemption* is a fundamental distrust of the hegemonic cultural megaphone that would obligate of all art a world-reparative function. "The catastrophes of history," he wrote then, "matter much less if they are somehow compensated for in art, and art itself gets reduced to a kind of superior patching function, is enslaved to those very materials to which it presumably imparts value." The injunction that art could somehow absolve the world of its calamity is a farce, one that Bersani points out is predicated on "a misreading of art as philosophy."[9] Art does not aspire to the realm of intelligible ideas, making any art that purports redemptive agency by a negation of the world itself, in Bersani's final analysis, a negation of art.

On this Lim is equally resolute: "The idea here," she writes alongside ethnomusicologist Joseph Browning, "is not that art can save the world."[10] *Extinction Events* does not purport to turn back the climate clock. Instead, it reaches toward something both far more modest and endlessly nobler:

> The role of art in the Anthropocene [is] in developing emergent forms of witnessing of, and lamentation for, the violence and losses of ecological harm, including the deep ambivalences involved in these necessary yet potentially harmful forms of attentiveness.[11]

Potentially harmful forms of attentiveness like the polycarbonate plastic that comprises a majority of the CD itself; or the thin case of polystyrene in which it comes packaged; the electrical energy expended in recording and mixing the album; the fossil fuels burned to transport it halfway across the world. *Extinction Events and Dawn Chorus* does not exempt itself from critique or speak as holier than thou. It only invites us to practice an expanded relationship with being-in-the-world that would mourn and acknowledge the contributions to ecocide in every effort to resist it. This is its sacred affordance, which isn't really an affordance at all: to return to objects the agency of thought beyond the limitations of the human, and to see all beings—past, present, and future—as inextricably and inexorably bound.

A question, after all, of what you believe an album can *do*.

Admission

In both senses of the word, an entry ticket by way of a confession. There are expectations for a book like this, things it's meant to promise. Musical biography, for one. Better listening, for another. Expertise, perhaps. Certainly conclusions.

I make no such promises. Not, of course, because they are unworthy, nor even unimportant; dogged historicism has a knack for turning up those thin threads of contingency that, when plucked, incite the great narratives of economy, nation, identity, and culture to rumble. There is, somewhere, a very interesting book to be had about how a music written from the wide-eyed vista of Australia's fragile position in the warming global basin, a music with vestiges of Ancient China and nineteenth-century Czechoslovakia and modern Hawai'i swept inside it, gets played and recorded at the teetering edge of a pandemic by a band of Austrians who are conducted by a German. Such a book might read the permissive omnivorousness of such a music—and the disparate bodies memorialized by its recording—as a strange mimetic doubling of the perverse global togetherness furnished by what Dipesh Chakrabarty calls the "emergent, new universal history of humans that flashes up in the moment of the danger that is climate change."[1] If this is not that book, it is in recognition of the fact that to ascribe stable conclusions—however noble and good and promissory—would be to entirely miss the point.

I wrote in the Introduction that *Extinction Events* belongs to a phase of Lim's music during which the application of sustained ecological thought to compositional practice becomes her primary occupation. (There's a long-since-outmoded musicological idea called *organicism* that likened musical development to entelechy, the self-generating growth of plants; Lim's ecological project can, in some senses, be thought of as a posthumanist reopening of that case.) The seed of that phase was planted by her encounter with Kohn's *How Forests Think*, in which the case is made for a more distributed and attendant appreciation of all the ways our thinking and dreaming is met by a natural world that thinks and dreams in reply, what Kohn calls an "anthropology beyond the human." The musical influence of Kohn's thought shows up in earnest with Lim's work (and, later, album) of the same name.[a] But of all her music from this verdant decade, *Extinction Events* is something like the *mise en abyme*. (And the *abyme*, the *abyss*, will return throughout this book as a frequent figure, the piece almost entirely comprised of folds into which the listener falls.) Where the material of neighboring works is influenced *by* ecological thought, *Extinction Events* is in many ways the diagram of that very thinking, an account of the pressures to experience and theory that ecocide poses, and an exercise in habituating thought to the consequences of an insurmountable fault-line called "our last day on earth." The other works are ecological; *Extinction Events thinks* ecological.

One of Kohn's provocations in that book is that ecological thinking requires us to forgo our human proclivity for stable, symbolic interpretation. That is, if we're always modulating music into some higher narrative or signification, we miss what is learned by keeping thought "close to the ground." Kohn recounts the story of Luisa, a Runa woman from Ecuador's

---

a Lim went on to co-teach a seminar on ecological thought with Kohn at the Banff Centre for Arts and Creativity in 2019.

Upper Amazon debating with a friend the portents of a birdcall that came moments before a jaguar attack. Unlike her friend, who reaches comfortably for the bird's social symbols, Luisa sends her language flying out to mimesis, echoing what she actually heard and allowing it to spill homophonically with other words to discover something "meaningful without necessarily meaning something." "When thought's 'purpose of yielding a return' is removed," Kohn writes, "what is left is that which is ancillary to or beyond what it is practical: the fragile but effortless iconic propagation of self-organizing thought, which resonates with and thereby explores its environment."[2] This, he suggests, is the checkered thought needed if we ever wish to account for, and not just explain away, the thinking and dreaming of other species, other worlds.

Félix Guattari, in his book on eco-philosophy, proposed three interlocking registers, three *ecologies* he called them, which, together, comprise the registers in which environmental catastrophe must be assessed and, someday, confronted: the environment itself, social relations, and human subjectivity.[3] The first two are, in the arena of Liza Lim, fairly epistemic. We can name, recount, and know all the found objects, the mimetic mappings of oceanic swirls, and tactics of architecture and sociality within ensemble coordination and performance. Environment and social relations are, here, just informational. But the quantity of human subjectivity, of *experience and interpretation*, is less known. For as a work of art, *Extinction Events and Dawn Chorus* demands an engagement by a listening Other who completes its ecology of thought. It *is* in being heard. As such, there remain a number of discrete moments on the album in which *how we listen* is inseparably tangled up in *what we hear*. It is these moments to which the following analysis gravitates, precisely because of the challenges they pose to writing. Staying with the trouble of thinking where you can't gives us what Donna Haraway called *speculative fabulations*,[4] and it is in Haraway's shadow that Lim posited perhaps her greatest legacy for the field of New Music, the one from which it can no longer turn away: her music exposes once and for all that not only is all interpretation already a kind of fiction but the conceding of our faith in empiricism is the first and necessary charter for any ethical—not to mention really, properly literate—New Music discourse.

The book in your hands, then, is decidedly anti-historicist, precisely for the reason that it attempts to answer with an impossible fidelity the call for commensurate thought this music sends out. In striving to do so, it must necessarily foreclose on affordances, any yieldings of return. There is no promissory attachment that we must "know this music better" as a result of the time spent here. In fact, the opposite is more likely, that we will only be more certain that there are things we cannot, should not, safely know. Stanley Cavell's famous diagnostic—that "the possibility of fraudulence, and the experience of fraudulence, is endemic in the experience of contemporary music"[5]—is both the field's limiting factor and its radical freedom: we do not have to barter success in advance; we couldn't, even if we wanted to. But we spend the time anyway, which, after all, is precisely this album's wager: that accepting the possibility of a no-yield bargain is in fact a very good place for ethical thinking to begin …

—except. Except there *are* a few facts you should know, especially if you come to this without them primed and close at hand. For instance, the fact that Lim was born in Perth to Chinese parents but raised in Brunei before being sent to boarding school at the Presbyterian Ladies' College in Melbourne, a trilogy of displacement that will unsettle her music from the first. Salman Rushdie described emigration as sometimes straddling two worlds, sometimes falling "between two stools,"[6] and while Liza Lim has never written "biographical" music, it is helpful to know that she has always understood the stable ground of "home" as a mirage: the vertigo of imperfect balance and always-about-to-fall *is* her sense of self. Likewise, she is—and I do not say this lightly—an *ethical* composer. As a member of the Australasian Diaspora, she has always sided her project with the colonized, writing music as a means for sounding out the sites where musical logic might unwind or foil the thinking patterns of empire. She maintains a feminist bent in her work both inside and outside the concert hall. Politics aside, she is also a fearsome and storied theorist of her own work.

The album in question, meanwhile, is collated from three discrete concert pieces: *Axis Mundi* (2013), for solo bassoon; *Songs found in dream* (2005), for nine musicians; and *Extinction Events and Dawn Chorus* (2018), for twelve musicians. *Extinction Events* in turn splits into five parts, which this book interchangeably refers to as both tracks and movements: (i) Anthropogenic Debris, (ii) Retrograde Inversion, (iii) Autocorrect, (iv) Transmission, and (v) Dawn Chorus. Our primary attention here will remain with the eponymous work, the density and richness of which will require all our attention.

With that admitted, a note about admission. I continue to offer no securities about either the purchase of access or the accessibility of purchase. I think you'll find that inside, outside, and entryway have a slippery propensity to look an awful lot alike here.

… It is [a] praxic opening-out which constitutes the essence of "eco-art." It subsumes all existing ways of domesticating existential Territories and is concerned with intimate modes of being, the body, the environment or large contextual ensembles …

—Félix Guattari, *The Three Ecologies*

When the paths traced out become too difficult, or when we see no path, we can no longer live in so urgent and difficult a world. All the ways are barred. However, we must act. So we try and change the world, that is, *to live as if the connection between things and their potentialities were not ruled by deterministic processes, but by magic.*

—Jean-Paul Sartre, *The Emotions: Outline of a Theory*

The point is rather that a spell needs a target, a subject who receives the spell—in nefarious cases a guileless listener, in beneficent ones a listener often caught off guard but invariably transfixed, *swept away*.

—Martha Feldman, "Vocal Deliriums (Five Proposals)"

Extinction Events and Dawn Chorus

Part I: Songs

(forever on their way to magic)

First as tragedy, then as farce: the echo always in variation, the difference always mattering. The greatest trick mankind ever played was in convincing itself that magic could be reasoned out of the world. The virtuosic sleight of hand by which the Enlightenment installed scientific rationalism involved a magician's art of distraction, dispelling magic and symbolic thought with a universal taboo forged in the doctrine of objectivity, only to redeploy the techniques it outwardly disavowed—"A look through the portal of science affects passionate spirits like the magic of all magic"[1]—in the policing of its absolute dominion.[2] For who among us would truly admit to experiencing that "magic hour" of the setting sun as the incremental turning of the Earth upon its axis? No matter with what certainty we see the sinking sun, we have been taught to remind ourselves the opposite: we do not see what we see. *Eppur si muove*, a legerdemain for the ages. And in a bizarre mimetic redoubling two centuries too late, the Enlightenment game plan makes a last-ditch cameo, only this time *ad absurdum*: postwar New Music, traumatized by the dazed mass choreography of an entire nation Sieg Heiling to Wagner in the Königsplatz, banished the category of *song* from its practices and raised on its shoulders the anesthetizing *work*.[3] And like the Enlightenment, which it so studiously copied, its crowning achievement was in believing that nature would never come back to haunt it.

You see, *song* was problematic for postwar New Music for the hallucinogenic surfeits it failed to fence in. Chase the word back far enough and you arrive at the Latin *cantare, to sing*, which, when combined with the prefix *in-*, becomes *incantare*, or *enchantment*: *song*, always one sound away from *magic*.[a] The mesmeric, the captivating, and the erotic were categories of deep anxiety for musical rationalism, which feared the short walk between collective ecstasy and fascist ideology. Which is not to say the Modernists didn't sing, quite the contrary; only the singing in question aspired to a "higher" category of objective coherence through the continuous effacement of its own enchanting embodiment. When Ernst Roth titled Richard Strauss's posthumous collection *Four Last Songs*, he could not have known just how apt that moniker was.

But no erasure is complete, not really. There were traces, bits of song-magic that bubbled up now and again to trouble the illusion of a hard-won rationalist surface. For a long while they came by way of historical citation, composers making copies of old music on the sly, as if the only way to safely commune with dangerous spirits was to hedge them into the box of parody and pastiche. Then ritual became a field-wide fascination, all secret theaters and invisible forces venting the pressure of repression. Gradually, factions began to split from the objectivists, with whole sects of composers defecting back

---

[a] Myth, literature, and history have habituated us to that danger through the female-coded figure of the *siren*; think also of Orpheus and his lyre taming death, or the anxiety-inducing female "voice beyond sense" that propelled the first Enlightenment reforms in opera.

to more "enchanting" musical vocabularies, while in America hypnotism went hip. Slowly but steadily, magical thinking[b] crept back into New Music, prompting Helmut Lachenmann to make his 2006 ultimatum: "This is the quandary: magic as a medium of familiar safety, even of irrational collective ecstasy, or magic as a medium of reflection, dominated and 'suspended' by a creative spirit?"[4]

Lachenmann saw a choice had to be made. His specter of "irrational ecstasy" compassed much more than some mere one-sided reproach of uninterrogated pleasurability. By Lachenmann's measure, *any* mindless adherence to stylistic hegemony, whether "blindly technical and empiricist" or nostalgic anachronist, was guilty of fascism's irrational and ecstatic groupthink.[5] One must "dominate" that magic spell of compliance, he says—the word is confounding at first pass. Isn't domination precisely the problem he's opposing? But the original German *beherrschte* is a hint, and following it plunges us headfirst back to magic. The word generally means *rule* or *control*, but in the context of music is more frequently rendered as *mastered*, as in an instrument or a phrase. Here Lachenmann begins to vibrate in tune with the anthropologist Michael Taussig, whose own theory of magic hinges on what he calls the "skilled revelation of skilled concealment": "exposure of the trick is no less necessary to the magic of magic than its concealment," Taussig says.[6] There is no magic, in other words, without the showing of the secret that there is no magic: the best magicians reveal that secret *as secret*. Taussig will later draw such patterned imperfection under the broadband of what he calls (the telling phrase) the "mastery of non-mastery"; skepticism of the trick is the trick's technique.[7]

---

[b] Which, let's clarify, is distinct from some impossible category of magical material; magic here is a question not of *what* but of *how*.

Beherrschte, then, in the context of Lachenmann, is better translated as the *mastery of non-mastery*, "breaking" the magic to strengthen it, the disarmament of one's own blind assurance in the same instant one pulls a rabbit out of a hat. Magic is this paradox, both *that which is intruded upon*—musical techniques of familiar safety, whether beautiful or rational—*and* the rebounding revelation of those interrupted techniques as newly animate, newly strange: "To break the magic in music," Lachenmann clarifies, "means to interrupt or, rather, to suspend its irrational power by intervening in the sounding structure of the magical object, thus provoking us to attend closely and intensely to what really is going on in our perception."[8] In this he echoes Victor Turner, who read in Indigenous monsters the function of "[startling] neophytes into thinking about objects, persons, relationships, and figures they had hitherto taken for granted."[9] Aesthetic rupture is passivity's antagonist; the skeptic leaning in to ask "what did I just hear?" provides magic's foundation.

If Lachenmann got anything wrong, then, it was only what he imagined the catalyst to be. His injunction stemmed from a fundamentally Marxist anxiety, a distrust of artistic production under a commodity capitalism that, in the twenty-first century, had ossified to frightening proportions. He presumed it would be economic precarity that forced New Music's hand. But by then, the sanctity of Nature—which had, in Germanic thought, long been considered the source of "creative spirit"—could no longer be taken as given. By then the meteorologist Paul Crutzen had already suggested that the irreversible role of mankind on geology and ecology had altered the makeup of the Earth enough to warrant a new epicycle, and with it a new name. Crutzen called it the *Anthropocene*, the age of irreparable human-made change on the Earth and its atmosphere. Donna Haraway later spun the term out to also include the Capitalocene,[10] nodding to Lachenmann that global economies are inseparable from environmental crises. But the real existential threat to New Music, the force prompting it to interrogate the theory of magic to which it ascribed, was not, in the end, economy: it was and remains ecology.

For both the dregs of Enlightenment culture and the dregs of New Music rationalism, environmental catastrophe is an ideologic nightmare. Both hedged their bets on a theory of nature as permanently controllable, the Enlightenment in its promise that man could govern the Earth on his own terms by overcoming the animal state, and New Music in its puritan belief that science could efface music of its "dirty" affective encrustations. But nature, caught up in our game of brinkmanship, is no longer behaving, prompting the Belgian chemist and philosopher Isabelle Stengers to rename Gaia "the one who intrudes."[11] According to Stengers, *intrusions* better characterize Earth's blind indifference to our excessive presence as she makes herself felt in response: the intruder does not knock politely, does not wait patiently for a convenient time. To insist that Gaia intrudes without asking for reply, that she is not conversationally considerate, is also to clarify the ways in which she is no longer ignorable. The intrusion of Gaia—Stengers's suggested nomination for the total assemblage of relations comprising "the living planet," that is *the being of planetary thought*[12]—is only the reminder that, as Stengers says, "we will have to go on answering for what we are undertaking in the face of an implacable being who is deaf to our justifications."[13] Catastrophe has made it impossible to forget that we are only entangled in, rather than sovereigns of, this world.

Entanglement castrates all those old Enlightenment command centers; Western colonial thinking is no longer adequate for surviving in this world. "The new dispensation [of climate catastrophe] propels bodily unconscious worlds into consciousness and vice versa," says Taussig: "Global warming alters the boundaries between mind and matter. *Knowing what not to know* [...] *is no longer autonomous*."[14] And here we get our first passing glimpse at the foundation of Liza Lim's current project: this catastrophe of the planet's thinkability with its aporias, estrangements, and anomalies has led contemporary eco-philosophy to the conclusion that Nature, pronounced as finally disenchanted back in 1788, is *re-enchanting* again. Strange things are happening, ecological upsets on a scale and impact for which human cognition and systemic thought have neither precedent nor model. Where humanity once safely labored under what Hartmut Rosa described as modernity's belief in "the world [as] engineerable, predictable, available, accessible, disposable in all its aspects,"[15] Gaia has forcefully returned the unknowable and unpredictable into our clean and balanced books: mystery is in again, the ghosts very much *in the system*. And while the technofuturists got busy proposing new and advanced models of predictive mitigation—all of which require more water, more energy, more infrastructure to "sustain"—the environmental philosophers, anthropologists, and cultural theorists have been insisting for some time on the reverse: that our best strategy for survival alongside an intruding Earth, the "art of living on a damaged planet," is to get practiced in falling again for magic.[16] It's too late for amnestic erasure of all our Enlightenment breakthroughs, but perhaps, as Taussig says, we can learn to know what not to know. Perhaps it's not so bad to imagine that the sun really does set, that "magic hour" really is the galactic fireworks of a star sinking into our ocean depths. (From Esperanza Spalding's lyrics to Wayne Shorter's "Endangered Species": "Though our science brought us to novel heights / We must come back to mother."[17]) The hope of reigniting our capacity for magic is not some misplaced nostalgia for a pre-literate time, nor does it harbor any conspiratorial suspicions of the astonishing advances that medicine and science have brought to bare living; instead, it is a bid to rewrite the ethics of how we think, feel, and act into our relationship with a planetary ecosystem in which it is no longer safe to assume we know what's best. Though he was referring to music, Lachenmann's earlier prescription was prescient: our survival in an intrusive, re-enchanted world is urgently dependent on our ability to recast magic as humanity's primary medium of reflection, a mimetic *mirror*, one in which to see ourselves see, hear ourselves hear, think ourselves think.

Taussig's *mastery of non-mastery* is a bid for precisely that philosophical reorientation through mimesis. His argument is a solar one: following thinkers like Nietzsche and Bataille, he takes the human to be a fundamentally sun-bidden creature, one whose taxic tropism with, toward, and around the mysterious ball of fire in the sky is evidence of a natural predisposition for imperfect mimesis—a recognition all the more urgent when it is precisely that life-giving sun stoking our endangerment. Taussig redirects us toward "magic hour," when the sun is just setting or rising, to note the blurry boundary-crossings between body and planets that happen there—and if his argument proves exceptionally tractional here, it is because a work whose final part is called *Dawn Chorus* is, in a very literal sense, an imagined tracery of how Anthropocentric boundaries will melt and morph in those last magic hours of the final human sunset. To practice the imperfect mimesis of non-mastery, Taussig says, is to get comfortable with the rapid interspecies and interplanetary relays that take place at magic hour: between my body and your body, your body and our body, the human body and the earthly body, the earthly body and the cosmic body, etc. *ad infinitas* is a flow of reflection and simulation without source. And that flow, Taussig says—"the facility with which soul can be dislocated from the body, implicating not one but several bodies flowing into and out of one another across borders accessed by dream, surrealism, and animal visitations"—that flow "*is in the song, the body of the song*."[18]

There is no singing on *Extinction Events and Dawn Chorus*: it is an album for instruments. But there is song: undoubtedly, there is song. The literal chorus of fish that croak and buzz in track five, the "Dawn Chorus" of the title, is, of course, the obvious contender. Lim loosely transcribed a recording made by oceanographers of schools of fish singing at sunrise off the coast of Australia's Port Hedland, replicating their waves of rasp through an intricate choreography of handheld drums.[c] Here is a chorus of singing; perhaps it is the song? But I want to resist the impulse to make of song a *thing that happens*, to cordon song into some safe, discrete event within the larger fabric of the album. Likewise, we should resist thinking song as only a structural index of the event of vocality, of singing, fishy or otherwise. (After all, I can sing without cohering into song.) Instead, I'd prefer we keep song radical—that is, etymologically speaking, *radix*, at the root—and leave it always on the

c Not for nothing is the blackspotted croaker, one of the fish heard on that recording, colloquially called a "drum."

ragged edge of magic. In place of event, the song would be only thought's scotoma, where the *skilled revelation of skilled concealment* convokes perception to attend to its own lack. What *enchants* could also be rewritten as what *ensongs*.

Song, then, is not singular but a capacious category of sound that suffuses all corners of *Extinction Events*. To find it, we need only retrace Lim's footsteps. The oldest work on the album, *Songs found in dream*, we have already said, is titled after an English approximation of the Kukatja word "kalyururu," whose alternative translation is "like water shimmering as it falls." Shimmer is the shibboleth. Lim's engagement with Aboriginal Australian art practices and philosophies in the early aughts[d] established the language for what she came to call an "aesthetics of presence," in which *shimmer*, the creation of stippled, flickering sound-surfaces gave the impression—virtual and yet undeniable—of a "beyond" or "invisible" dimension, another "presence" in the sound. In his now-classic essay on Lim's music, Tim Rutherford-Johnson defines "shimmer" as "a fine partitioning of the sound-continuum into an alternating on/off pattern, a simple musical analog for the cross-hatching of Yolŋu painting."[19] Rapid alteration creates a tremulous effect, a discontinuous fluttering of the veil between this world and that, enough that some *there* might just slip into our *here*—

—or at least that's how it usually goes. But we might apply a little pressure to Rutherford-Johnson's work and draw out some of the less obvious consequences shimmer has on the

[d] Shimmer is a widely recognized category of Australian Aboriginal aesthetics; Lim first encountered it in Howard Morphy's ethnography. See Morphy, *Ancestral Connections: Art and an Aboriginal System of Knowledge* (University of Chicago Press, 1991), 194.

task of written reception and interpretation. For Lim's attendant discourse, shimmer has primarily served as an access point to language. That she herself named it first has given writers and theorists the impression of an empirical foothold: "this exists and it matters." As a result, the interpretations generally deemed "successful" almost always involve a game of hide and seek, tracking down and describing all the places in any given work where shimmering appears. Rather than pursue a rigorous account of the *implications* of Lim's shimmer, however, her discourse has sated itself on shimmer's apparent liberal invitation to creative adjectives. Even in the paragraph above, we can see how tempting words like *tremulous, stippled, flickering, fluttering, destabilized,* and *discontinuous* become, how much interpretive purchase they appear at first to secure. I'm less convinced that shimmer is merely a texture to be described. That said, neither do I want to so quickly discount the impulse to taxonomize shimmer, because the very question at its root—"where is there shimmer?" or "what is shimmering?"—turns out to be an extraordinarily useful index for thinking what it is that shimmer does to listening.[e] If we attempt to say for certain that "this" or "that" particular passage is "shimmer," *to what exactly are we referring*? The sound, after all, is only a succession of much smaller and nonequivalent sounds of indeterminate quality, the isolation of any one of which would only reveal another folded layer of serration. To point to shimmer, then, is to name not a sound but a *surface*, a kind of textured surplus extrinsic to the sphere of sound

e Which, after all, is the question to which all music criticism needs answer: what does a given sound or event do to my capacity to make meaning with or alongside it in the act of auditory perception?

production (*surface* after all shares an identical etymology with *surfeit*). *Shimmer is a crisis of ontology*: it does not exist except in our perpetual reconstruction of so many discrete sounds, our intervening failure to separate effect from result. Or, following Taussig, we might describe it as a kind of trick of the ear: hearing one thing (a 'cello tremolo or some stuttering percussion), we perceive another sound, an effect of depth and dissimulation, which is to say we *perceive ourselves hearing more than we hear*.

We can take this further and say that what defines Lim's shimmer aesthetics is not a category of descriptive sound but a destabilization of the subject-object binary along which traditional listening occurs. That is to say: if the listener is inseparable from "making" shimmer (we turn the productive excess of the sound into an object; we index and give credence to something that is not strictly "on the page"), the listening subject is no longer separable from what it hears. Not for nothing does Taussig frame the visual effects of magic on near identical terms:

> This is not a question of seeing more or seeing less or seeing behind the skin of appearances. Instead, it turns on seeing how one is seeing. *Whatever magic is, it must involve* this turn within the known unknown and on what this turn turns on, namely, *a new attitude to skin.*[20]

Magic, like shimmer, involves a new attitude to skin, one whose constant recourse to exteriority and surface forces listeners to reconcile their own inseparable participation in the illusion of auditory perception. Likewise, Taussig's phrase recalls the art historian Mieke Bal's work on folds and the Baroque, which proceeds with what she calls a "hallucinatory obsession with surface, a texture it takes seriously as simply being all there is"[21]—and there is indeed something curiously

Baroque about Lim's highly ornamented surfaces of glistening texture. One of Bal's central theses—of which we'll see much more in Part III—is that the viewer of Baroque art is embroiled in meaning-making in ways that similarly unsettle any stable, authoritative subject. As with Stenger's Gaia, the art intrudes on the once-secure Cartesian subject, miring and unbinding it in an endless relay of continuous becoming. Earlier we said that shimmer has served as a kind of access point for thinking Lim's music, a portal of sorts. The phrase was unexpectedly apt: shimmer is the place where listening "falls into" the music, where it cannot but make meaning because it is already there in the making.

Let's briefly summarize. Postwar New Music resurrected the great playbook (it's actually more like a spell book) of Enlightenment to banish the magic of song. But song is inextricably bound to nature, and in a re-enchanting, intrusive, ecocidal world, the suppression of magic begins to look more and more like certain death. Philosophers and anthropologists insist: we need to get better at not mastering our mimetic dancing with the natural world, at recognizing all the things it's irresponsible to know, if only to entangle ourselves more ethically in the webs of ecological being. New Music was an early respondent to that re-enchanting call, returning shares of its relaying flow to the many participatory bodies in its creative economies.[f] While not the first, Liza Lim becomes the most visible composer to answer that imperative, working in

---

[f] Even if, at least then, it didn't recognize the source: the return of song-magic was heralded at different moments by different flags—decolonization, gender parity, aesthetic inclusivity, improvisation—the common thread of which was a demand for more ethical exchanges between bodies and the musical matter of earthly being; they were all, in some sense, ecological.

tandem with Indigenous thought and early ecological criticism to invest her music with a new category she calls shimmer: a magic trick of the ear whose skilled revelation of its skilled concealment draws the listener into active participation in its multi-bodied weaving of song.

We have established a kind of auditory kaleidoscope in which shimmer, magic, and song all begin to shuffle places. Now, perhaps, it's time to forge the link between all three. Lim wrote another piece in 2018, the same year *Extinction Events* debuted, a piece for solo woodblock called *An Elemental Thing* for which she also wrote an accompanying essay tellingly titled "How to Make a Woodblock *Sing*." The main wager of that piece involved rethinking how a woodblock "speaks." Where most composers treat it as a blunt object to be hit (it utters by being struck, best for single piercing sounds), she drew across it all manner of serrated implements, activating a kind of throaty croak from the woodblock's "mouth"—the hollow wooden slit carved into an otherwise simple hunk of material—that could then be manipulated by the percussionist's free hand. (The same way a tongue shapes the inside of a mouth to produce various vowels and consonants.) Player and instrument begin to combine, each extending the other until Rutherford-Johnson's "fine partitioning of the sound-continuum" takes on an uncannily *vocalic* quality and the surrogate mouth begins, improbably, to *speak*. Taking the effect to its extreme limit, Lim inscribed the score with a series of lines from Eliot Weinberger's "The Stars," asking the percussionist to shape the shimmering sound according to however they imagine the text might be spoken "in woodblock." The result? Here's Lim: "A humble piece of wood with a slit carved out to promote resonance, improbably becomes an orator, a body with a mouth that speaks of the stars."[22]

Now of course, it doesn't actually "speak," per se: what the listener hears is a series of highly variegated rasps that contain a kind of fluctuating interior pitch. We certainly don't perceive complete words, much less English syntax. But we cannot fail to register that some kind of vocalic utterance, perhaps even intelligible to a being who is not us, is issuing from the mouth of a drum. It is precisely that relay in which we invest a nonhuman object with expressive capacity despite both its imperfect achievement of those behaviors and our imperfect reception of their meaning which Taussig would say is *the mastery of non-mastery*. The trick isn't feigned by some electronic sleight of hand; neither does the human speak *for* it. Instead, the listeners—habituated as speaking humans with access to language—recognize something of themselves in a piece of wood, "hearing" a communication that, strictly speaking, never takes place. This is good old-fashioned magic, precisely because you can see exactly what's taking place *and yet still* hear something else: the *skilled revelation of skilled concealment*. "Somehow these nonhuman sounds made it into human language, altered but reasonably unscathed," Timothy Morton would say.[23] The spell is aided by the raspy woodblock's uncanny similarities to other songs of the animal kingdom, a likeness Lim has elsewhere used to her advantage: in the opera *Tree of Codes*, a collection of woodblocks congeal into an imagined frog chorus that "sings" Goethe's poem Erlkönig. (And here we can tighten the knot with magic by remembering that the chapter "Magic Birth" in Morton's book *Realist Magic*—one of Lim's favorites—opens with an extended meditation on frog choruses, in which the inability to name precisely what the song *is* constitutes the entire ethical challenge to the phenomenal status of objects.[24] Or else we could remember Taussig's suggestion that magic's flow of the body of the song is also "what is going on between animals and humans."[25] Or else remember Donna Haraway's insistence that pets are where we humans most clearly see our Otherness flowing into a more ethical being-with-nature.[26] Or . . .)

Most theorists of Lim's shimmer prefer the kind of glittering string and wind effects that, conveniently, also produce rather beautiful music. (See the ventilated bassoon trills that make track six, *Axis Mundi*, so gauzy.) But if we expand the definition to compass any ontological return to surface, we are permitted a more capacious and productive attention to these sites where listening falls continuously in the gap or rift, an endless becoming-object continually troubling subjecthood. Properly speaking, when one is shrouded in shimmer "one finds oneself in a world that does not exist, or that exists only in this space at this moment," in Jonathan Flatley's resonant phrasing. Flatley continues: "This otherness is not liberatory in itself, but inasmuch as the relationships between space and time, for example, that we are used to in our everyday lives are altered in some way or another, we may see that the logic of the world we live in is not compulsory. Things might work differently."[27] Shimmer, then—which, we should note, more than echoes with Theodor Adorno's shudder, that shock whose "patient contemplation" causes the artwork to "begin to move"[28]—inheres in the political imaginary, a dimension to which Lim herself has attended: "Meaning," she says of the "singing" in *An Elemental Thing*, "is [. . .] created in the contingency of the attentiveness of listeners [who] are actively making what they know through their own wideware." This, Lim continues, "is fundamentally an engagement that speaks to, with and through frameworks of political and cultural codes of power."[29] What shimmers is not a thing but a lack of one, the making-mirage of any boundary that might allow us to imagine an

I cordoned off from the world: shimmer is the opening to entanglement.

An Elemental Thing's discrete class of shimmer—the serrated percussion whose virtuosic guttural oration we hear as more-than-human song—permeates *Extinction Events and Dawn Chorus* almost from the first. Twenty seconds into the opening track, a Waldteufel—a percussion instrument native to many regions of the world but popularized under its German name, whose translation ("forest devil") hints at the magically animate and nonhuman quality of its sound—croaks a great yawn from under all that slippery brass. It enters alongside a bass clarinet trill that mimics its serration but is not itself entirely unprepared. The cat-and-mouse game played first by the brass settles around a half-step drone, causing both instruments to beat against the stabilized cello and the shadow of the bass clarinet. In hindsight, it is as if these rapid interferences in frequency—this ghostly acoustic phenomenon which belongs not to any single source but the surface interaction of several—produce their own tiny shimmer that uncorks the more powerful Waldteufel, which in turn summons other, literal voices into being: during the drum's nearly thirty-second span, the brass players, so clarion at the outset, begin to sing into their instruments, causing the whole apparatus to ghost and shake. Everything is always already there, time-spirals, folded up inside.

And while the Waldteufel maintains an ongoing identity of its own—it is the entire sonic premise for track five's "Dawn Chorus"—I want us to spin out some of the consequences of this earliest occurrence, and in particular what it does to both the instruments around it and the sounds that follow it. Like the brass, singing into their instruments to blur and "haunt" their previous pure tone, the serrated shimmer has a *revelatory* effect: it unconceals hidden dimensions of other instruments, binding them to its spell. A minute later, for instance, when the trumpet gets caught in its pleading repeat, it will be difficult to isolate the suddenly nasal cello drone underneath it from the slow and intermittent Waldteufel. (An effect replicated in track seven, *Songs found in dream*, where a rainstick hinges to a 'cello whose instruction reads: "gentle distortion (like rainstick)."[30]) Or later in the first track, when the brass put aluminum over their bells (for the recording it was to-go pizza containers!), adding a buzzy excess to the sound that disconnects from some essential "trumpet" or "trombone" and reattaches haphazardly to the drum. And in an excellent hint of foreshadowing, the extended first track violin solo, beginning rich with surfeit pressure to groan uncannily like a frog chorus and only later flying into virtuosic stratospheres when the drums themselves take over, prepares in reverse the magic trick in track four. What the piece does, in other words, is entrain us to hear all sounds on a spectrum of relative shimmer. It makes a kind of intuitive sense: if we recall that Lim writes music to activate the space between this world and invisible Others, shimmer becomes a default state of her music.[g] Shimmer has an amplitude factor on which one can map any instrumental utterance according to its degree of interference.

---

[g] The actual ascription she has given to her default is "distortion," for its suggestions of "a trace, the evidence of invisible presences squeezing through into our space-time field. Distortion brings strangeness, alien-ness, divine or demonic energies, shock, repulsion, awe and other signs of the sublime into view."[31] We can think of distortion as a discrete species of a broader genus, shimmer.

The idea is, in some senses, a rather old one. One of Karlheinz Stockhausen's definitive contributions to New Music's written thought was an essay called "... How time passes ...." There, he made the case that a complete system of compositional objectivity could be constructed from psychoacoustics by accepting the principle that pitch and rhythm exist on the same spectrum. He called it a timefield.[32] We can hear this intuitively in the Waldteufel, which, as it spins faster, approaches something like discrete pitch. Likewise, we refer to high sounds as "high frequencies" (which is inversely why subsonic frequencies register to us as a kind of rhythmic thudding; see Part IV for the consummation of that principle). Stockhausen's suggestion was that one could rationalize all compositional events by relating pitch's micro-time to rhythm's macro-time, constructing a system in which all elements cohere in a utopian harmony of vibrational periodicity: the complete control of nature. Lim's, then, is the riposte of re-enchantment to Stockhausen. She takes the fundamental principle—that the nature of sound exists on a spectrum which necessarily includes information at extremes which the brain does not experience as phenomena but which are nevertheless both *there* and *employable*—and unwinds it of its Nietzschean will to power, recasting the absences not as knowable, calculable entities but as precisely what cannot be accounted for. Granting autonomy to the destabilizing forces—pizza pans and singing trumpets and violins under duress cannot act in predictable, controllable ways—she refuses to subjugate under a reigning Anthropocentrism what are in Stockhausen's theory the more-than-human or superhuman variables. Regular pitch production becomes, in Lim's schema, no longer some imagined "purity" (the human as the "perfected" animal, stripped of all the aberrations that make Otherness inferior) but merely an arbitrary landing strip between posthuman extremes of perception and articulation. By the end of the track, all instruments have been recontextualized as gradated instantiations according to the fundamental shimmer of the drum. Here, then, is where most theorists of shimmer go wrong: it is not a question of shimmer and its negative, some virtual alternative against which shimmer posits itself; it is rather a question of amplitude, *everything* as shimmer, merely more or less.

This remains true even in the most traditional of the tracks. "Autocorrect" is a hallucinogenic production of historical residues. Lim herself has said that the many almost tonal chords in that movement contain calculated grain to give them something of a flicker: "the radiant beauty of sonorous chords is mixed with many impurities that *make one aware* of the alienated nature of the harmonic borrowing."[33] Lim is practicing a rather acute version of Lachenmann's prescription to interrupt the irrational spell of music by revealing its magic so that we are provoked "to attend closely and intensely to what really is going on in our perception."[34] For Lachenmann as for Lim, those interrupted imperfections create their own, new kind of conscious magic. The imperfections, then, are a kind of shimmer. In these most objective, indexable moments of the work—when the echo of traditional classical music seems almost (but it really is almost, never quite congealing) to bubble up—the intentional aberrations (slight detunings, odd voicings, weird fingerings) keep us closely attuned to the surface and to our own, endangering involvement in the illusion of historicity.

But it is in track four that the spectrum is laid most bare, now with all the expressive force of a classroom drama. "Transmission" is—breaking from the dense ensemble writing elsewhere on the album—a duet, for the solo violinist who has been a continuously disruptive force in the previous three tracks and a single percussionist.[h] When the work is performed live, the pair will break off from the ensemble to approach the front of the stage, where a desk—often outfitted with lamp and music stand, a kind of domestic reading space—is already prepared: for the sake of the album, it helps to imagine them, newly separate from the rest of the players and lit in a kind of mini theater, an odd couple if there ever was one. The violinist brings their—often very expensive and familiar—instrument along, while the percussionist picks up a much-more-roughshod tool at the desk: a snare drum, whose head has been threaded with a thin string, the extreme end of which is affixed with a small handle, turning the once-familiar drum into a monstrous hybrid string instrument that sings with a strange skin "throat." The percussionist then, too, picks up a bow, completing the eerie and imperfect resemblance of the historically flawless violin standing by its side.

First, there's tuning, and there will continue to be: Lim instructs the violinist to repeatedly interrupt her playing to check the tuning of the instrument, simulating—or is it a simulation if she is, indeed, testing calibration each time?—a kind of low-fi practice session. When the violin finally begins to play, it is a high, anfractuous (dare we say Romantic?) line, winding and weaving before throwing itself skyward in a repeated, heaving figure. The solo is short—maybe a minute at most?—but hardly simple. Plenty of sliding and difficult

---

[h] Here Sophie Schafleitner, violinist for Klangforum Wien since 1997, and Lukas Schiske, one of the ensemble's founding members.

double-stops attest to an absolute mastery of the instrument.[i] This is a virtuoso demonstration, to be certain, but not without its flaws: all the obsessive repeats suggest practice sessions, a going-over-it-alone. It ends without settling, expectant.

The drum begins. At first, we barely recognize the similarity. The snare, metamorphosed into a kind of monstrous Waldteufel—Lim has a special affinity for hybrid instruments, which, like the Turner essay cited above, estrange formerly familiar musical bodies and startle us into seeing them anew—takes on much the same qualities as the shimmering percussion found elsewhere on the album. It is a long, confusing moment of tracking the vertiginous swoops of guttural emission before it clicks: the drum is—improbably!—singing the violin line; or, *how to make a snare drum sing*. Absent all the hardware necessary for its virtuosic agility, the drum is nevertheless hazarding a *non-mastery* of the song, and though it sings nothing close to the gossamer pitches of its teacher, we reconstruct the likeness anyway through a mixture of memory and investment. In doing so—and here that familiar relay of shimmer reappears—we "complete it," transforming the ungainly sweeps and rasps into a song through a quantity of our attention and imagination. Magic broken—it sounds at first like a bad parody—as magic regained—the alienated shock: a drum is singing.

The violin recommences, this time with more filigree and with a wonderful trill on which it pours an ample amount of attention. The drum replies, more scrupulous now, though

i Much of the material is borrowed from another now-classic "shimmer" solo, *The Su Song Star Map* for solo violin, it, too, premiered—what a year—in 2018; more on borrowing in Part II.

when it comes to the trill, the violin cuts in with a "correction," as if *teaching* some technique or special trick. (Again, what is theater here? A percussionist has none of a violinist's string training, so perhaps the showing of a finger motion or a bow angle, though scripted, isn't really a performance? Perhaps the percussionist has, indeed, something to learn? Is this a simulacrum of pedagogy or an example of it?) The drum repeats the lesson and moves on to complete the passage. And we, now certain of what is taking place, hear "better" the imperfect mimesis. The percussionist is no less accurate than before, only our listening is different now: we hear our own ability to hear what first was alien.[J] Silence again.

And now, so long awaited, the duet proper. That their song is so evidently intended as a unison is a feat of skilled musicianship: even Lim herself admits astonishment at the "phenomenal level of rhythmic and gestural accuracy" achieved on the album, prompting one to "almost forget" the limitations of the drum's mimesis.[35] But the key-word there is *almost*: this is still an old-fashioned trick of puppetry, a ventriloquist's act in which the questions "who is singing?" and "who is playing who?" enter into relay, shimmering all the way down. Ventriloquism is the skilled revelation of skilled concealment par excellence: I know it's a puppet, I know who is speaking, *and yet I cannot help but hear and see that* … The projective confusion between viewer/listener and performer/result on which ventriloquism rests is outlined in clearest form

J The effect was prepared in some senses by the long cello solo at the end of "Retrograde Inversion," where we hear the pitched material go "underwater" through the gradual increase of pressure but retain a ghostly capacity to track shadows of those once-familiar notes.

in Steven Connor's history of the art, in a passage pregnant with ecological resonances:

> The audience is made to hear the voices not from their seats but from the position of the performer, into which they are expected to have transposed themselves. It would seem, in fact, that imagining something requires a kind of bodily projection into and participation in what is being imagined, so that, far from imagination overriding or contradicting the operations of mimicry, [...] *imagination may depend upon the propensity to sympathetic imitation*. Imagining might therefore involve mimicry in just the same way as mimicry involves imaging—the impressing of an image upon the body.[36]

Just as Taussig suggested that the flow of magic's non-mastered technique between bodies is best instantiated in song, so too does this longest "transmission" see bodies enter into multidirectional relays of fluid technical exchange. The violin part is newly gritty and unpredictable in places, multiphonics and overpressure bringing it far closer to the snare drum than first impressions suggested it ever could be. (We do not say often enough how much teachers learn from their students.) The drum, meanwhile, has proved itself not an equal so much as an expert in getting close, a master in non-mastery.

Then the *coup de théâtre*: the last two minutes of the track involve no drum at all. One would think, perhaps even expect, that the snare, taught to "sing," would break into a solo all of its own, leaving the violin behind as it embarks on a future of auto-emission. A redemptive composer would have offered autonomy as the reward for all that practice. But the twist is that the snare earns nothing for its labor. The teacher remains alone. Lim, for her part, has suggested a few readings of the moment: "perhaps the violinist has 'won' the competition," she says, "or perhaps the snare-drum has, leaving the violin to its doleful self"; she even hints that "here, recurrences translate into uncertainty."[37] But I want to offer another reading, one that puts the notion of supplementarity back into the context of both magic and a nonredemptive ethics for entangling with a re-enchanted world. Amid the many inter-body relays established in "Transmission" (the title suggesting all manners of infective vector), we have already said the violin teaches the drum to sing, and teaches us to hear the drum as *ensonged*, and that the drum in turn teaches the violin new ways of singing; we have not yet accounted for what the drum teaches us.

The duet is the consummation of our spectrum of shimmer: it is the ultimate magic trick, showing precisely how it works even as our ears fall for the illusion of a drum singing in perfect unison. Our inability to adequately distinguish one from the other—Taussig's flow between local and celestial bodies being played out in small scale[k]—causes the shock of recognition. The necessity of investment on the part of the listener is a habituation of precisely the kind of ethical non-mastered being-with-nature for which *Extinction Events* is making the case.

If the drum has achieved anything, it is these small impressions on the violin carried over the fault line of the

---

[k] Compounded when we recall that violin's material is extrapolated from a solo piece in which the very premise of the work is a translation of a speculative mapping of time and the heavens by a eleventh-century Chinese scientist into the language of the violin, a string instrument "reading" the map of light that is no longer there.

drum's absence. Accordingly, the net of deconstructive repeat signs—more on these in III—that glitch and whorl the flow of this music should not be read as failure or uncertainty. They are, rather, the auditory vacuum left by the taking-leave of any human subjectivity that would connect musical utterance into some greater, historical grammar. As in the Kohn anecdote from "Admission," this is a meaningful music without necessarily meaning *something*: that it refuses to cohere is not evidence of its shortcoming but of a logic of epicycle that postdates symbolic intervention. But even in that sound, there will be traces of a lost humanity, impressions left on the species that survive. How many mimicking birds will chirp half-remembered echoes of the anthropogenic soundscape long after we are no longer here?

Though there will be several, here is our first *mise en abyme*: we bear witness to a minor act of pedagogy in the mastery of non-mastery, pedagogy that goes on even as the final moments of humanity are secured, even as the posthuman Dawn Chorus prepares its intolerable, inexorable, irreversible arrival in the encroaching darkness behind. This minor pedagogy is an ethics of survival pressing on, even at the bitter last.

We are all of us this drum.

A GRAFT or AN ADJACENCY or A PORTICO

"This is our misfortune: in the case of apocalypse—when we are invited to rise above ourselves, so as to see the worst, as though to see the best—almost always we faint away. Mourning shows us the door, we are dislodged from our interior habitation, an absence moves in our place.

[…]

"However prepared we are, we are *never prepared*."[38]

Part II: Found

(and ever lost again: on skin)

> *There are traces of an outside afloat within this album, things over which it cannot lay full authorial claim. What to do, what to make, of what is by foreignness found?*

Plastered to Jack Whitten's 1990 *Door to Manhattan* is a spendthrift collection of pressed and trodden things. With the title in mind, the mess rather easily reads as an agglutinated catalog of discarded New York symbols: geometric outlines replicating in the folds of wire mesh, squashed metal amidst the imprints of bricks and manhole covers, bottle bottoms. In a particularly *Extinction-Events*-worthy proximity, a pair of fish swim toward a cassette tape (Figure 1). At first glance, the refuse appears grafted to the surface by the thick layer of monochrome silver, as if acrylic paint had rebranded as a superior kind of resin. But things are not exactly as they seem. Whitten, recovering from a studio fire in 1980 that left him without a space in which to work, had to revise the very function of paint itself. Plaster in hand, he sought instead objects and outlines from the streets around him, bringing home molds of various nondescript items that he could later fill with acrylics that would dry into sculptural reliefs. Where at first glance one sees a tangled mess seemingly fused to the door by paint itself, the reality is of a mere surface, pressed with the imprint of things now lost. Accordingly, *Door to Manhattan* is cataloged as only "acrylic on canvas": there is no door to speak of, though with the canvas providing the illusion of depth, you certainly could have fooled me.

Figure 1 *Jack Whitten,* Door to Manhattan *(1990) © 2025 Jack Whitten Estate/Artists Rights Society (ARS), New York. Photo by Christopher Stach.*

One wonders, then, what to call the fish and the cassette tape, the bottle bottoms, and the mesh. What I mean is that they can't properly be called objects, but they're something more than representations too. The door is closer to a *trope l'œil* that promises the original cassette as still there if only you could scratch off enough of the paint, except of course there's nothing to be **found** [past particle from the German *finden*, to *discover* or *perceive by chance*] underneath but paint itself. The painting is—and here Whitten unconceals some fundamental truth about painting in general—an impression, a shell of the world. Laying bare the space of absence left behind by a once-present object is, of course, a well-trod practice for modernity. But this is not quite the same, because absence is not what is first given to attention. Neither can they properly be called "**found** objects" in the old Duchamp sense, though that is indeed their simulation. They maintain, however fragile, a status of reproduction; the original is elsewhere. And so what are they?

The answer will lie in a sequence of anterooms, traced by a double motion: unbearable closeness to the door (we never enter) through a series of backward steps. Best, though, to start with an account of that inaccessible center, the very thing this refuse is cast on—or is it as?

When Goethe, alongside Johann Heinrich Meyer, **founded** [that is, *established*, *set place*, *fashioned*, from the Latin *fundus* for *bottom*, *foundation*] a journal for the dissemination of ideas about art and aesthetics, he called it *Propylaea*, from the Greek for *entryway*. He wrote an introduction to the first issue (an entryway to the entryway, we might say) that opened (the entryway to the entryway to the entryway, as it were) with the following:

> THE youth, when Nature and Art attract him, thinks that with a vigorous effort he can soon penetrate into the innermost sanctuary; the man, after long wanderings, finds himself still in the outer court.
>
> Such an observation has suggested our title. It is only on the step, in the gateway, the entrance, the vestibule [which is not quite accurate; the original is *Tor*, the *gate* or *door*], the space between the outside and the inner chamber, between the sacred and the common, that we may ordinarily tarry with our friends.
>
> [...] The name of the place may be understood as symbolizing what might have happened there; one may expect *conversations and discussions* such as would perhaps not be unworthy of that place.[39]

And so the unopened door hinges two otherwise dissimilar spaces: that of a maturated responsibility (which is to say, noninvasive and nontotalizing) in thinking art and nature, and the vista of conversation. An unlikely pair, it's true, but with the Whitten still in our sights it begins to make a kind of sense. Whitten's door is not, does not open: we stand before it in the anterior space of entry, permanently having-not-yet-been-admitted. Nor is it open in an interpretive sense, that is to say it does not bare or denude complete objects under the sign of the accessible concept. The true *objet trouvé*, the true found object, is an already open portal to another space, another time, one actively invited to be accessed. In Whitten's case, the door—the symbol of access—remains closed, in that one cannot "get at" or re-find the objects themselves. Any attempt to cleave it leaves one faced only with paint, stuck still outside the work (there is no "under" or "behind" to "get at").

In other words, one can only retain what is "behind" the door—the virtual *there* of which every door is always an expression—as an unknowable quantity toward which to think. That retention accepts the bargain that the *there* in question (in Goethe, "Nature and Art") will remain an alterity. Levinas would call this orientation without affordance a "relation with the Other," one he also deems as "ethical."[i] And here we take our first step back so as to move in the same gesture toward Goethe and the door, because Levinas has another word for this relation, this continuous being-towards-what-is-not-me that the inaccessibility of Whitten's *Door* demands: "the relation with the Other," he says, can also be called "*Conversation*."[40] Here Avital Ronell takes the phone to extrapolate:

> Conversation is not that which fuses you to me; but the experience of Conversation induces, once again, the vertigo of expropriation. It is not only the case that I am not identical to myself when I begin to converse with you, but more severely, perhaps: you are no longer the one I have interiorized or memorized. [...] Something else occurs between us, and I cannot say it is altogether you, it's not you and me but something else still.[41]

Not for nothing does Ronell's *something else still* carry a whiff of the violin-snare duo. If conversation as ethical relation always involves the acknowledgment that my conversation partner is *different and more than I can know*, it stands to reason

---

i One is reminded of ecological thinking's imperative for an "ethics beyond the human," one founded on the desertion of any and all totalizing knowledges (except, of course, the total knowledge that there should be no total knowledges, Taussig's *mastery of non-mastery*, a rather excellent *mise en abyme* if ever there was one).

that every conversation contains a deposition of surfeit, of excess. Levinas ties this excess to what he sees as the *pedagogic* nature of Conversation: "inasmuch as it is welcomed this conversation is a teaching [. . .], it comes from the exterior and *brings me more than I can contain*."[42] A teaching which is also an unmanageable excess is precisely what takes place in the unison transmissions, when both players come uncannily to resemble (*re-semblance*, as if recalling a likeness buried within but long forgotten) the other without ever actually fulfilling that moving-towards. (And that's before we remember that in the structure of the work, "Transmission" stands on the threshold, the anteroom of the instant of human extinction.) When Goethe suggested that the space before the door was the worthiest for conversation, he inadvertently invested a kind of ventriloquist's power upon the door itself, a compulsion it effects to bind those before it into magical, invisible relation. He was later answered in that by Sigmund Freud, who, explaining psychoanalysis to a distrustful layman, admitted frankly that "nothing takes place between [analyst and patient] except that they talk together." To which the layman responded with relief: "So it is a kind of magic."[43]

Here we step back again to find another antechamber. In 1917, Marcel Duchamp, tired of tripping over a coatrack he left lying on the ground ("I would kick it every minute, every time I went out," he recalled,[44] suggesting that it was the coatrack's invasive presence *just before the door* that was most irritating), went and nailed the offending item to the floor as punishment, bestowing upon this new Readymade the name of *Trébuchet*, or *Trap* (Figure 2). Many ways to read that title: we might ask Who is trapped? (The coatrack? The clumsy artist? The viewer striving to make meaning from it?) or else think about the *trébuchet* as chess move (a game with which he was

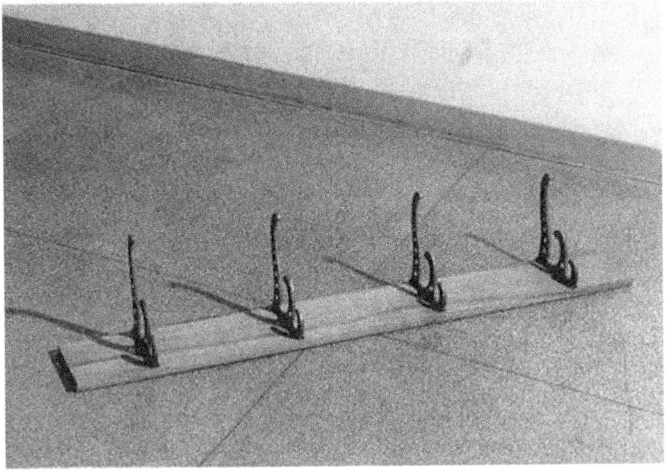

Figure 2 *Marcel Duchamp,* Trébuchet *(1917/1964) © Association Marcel Duchamp/ADAGP, Paris/Artists Rights Society (ARS), New York 2025.*

obsessed). But I merely want to tarry in the formal foyer of the work. What we have is a found object whose closure—traps are merely blueprints of potential until they're set in motion, and thus require successful activation by prey to maintain their status; we assume, if the title holds, that Duchamp's *Trap* is a successful one, that it has or is always already snapping shut—releases a discursive excess: entrapment (being nailed to the floor) brings art out of the lowly coatrack.

In her figuration of the trap, Rey Chow seizes on precisely this sudden secretion of excess at the instant of Duchamp's nailing-in, what she calls "a supplementary plane of articulation" that appears at the moment of capture. This supplement, she explains, only comes from a more expansive theorizing of entrapment that more ethically accounts for the prey's hallucinogenic and nonreducible experience of being trapped:

> Such discursive excess means that *a supplementary plane of articulation*, the plane of articulation of an other, ensnared in but not coinciding with the hunter's [...] and oscillating between the shock of ensnarement and the pain of possible annihilation, now slides into place to rupture, from within, the trap's presumed discursive unity. Entangled, vulnerable, and delirious, this supplementary discursive plane come into being—"appears," as it were—only as the trap snaps shut, yet has the potential of tilting the trap *towards a radically heteronomous affective assemblage*.[45]

Later she will ascribe capture's heteronomy to the "reciprocation of the hailing of an alterity" inherent to it, and in doing so will intimately recall Levinas's Conversation (and who among us has never before felt *trapped* in a conversation, whether as hostage or as entangled, enthusiastic participant who could not bear to stand up from the table?). Prey is the Other of hunter, who, in setting the trap, asks to be Othered in return. What is so particular about the form of the trap's exchange is that its excess is produced by the loosening or losing of the self by *one* party, not both. That loosening—Chow clarifies, and recalling the figure of the door as she does so—"is *not the result of crossing an external border or overcoming a constraint*; rather, it occurs from within the limits imposed by the situation."[46] Which is to say that from within the very experience of being trapped, something leaks from the prey which is neither anticipated nor accounted for in the trap itself but which nevertheless transforms its affective ontology. (And entrapment isn't always a negative valence; we desire to be captivated by art, for example, or by nature. Or by love.) To be trapped is to be flooded with this excess: I am Other to/prey of/outside you.

Let's retrace our steps. Standing outside of Whitten's *Door* and mired in the enterprise of determining its various ontological statuses (is it a painting? a found object? an impression? a trick of the eye?), we heard Goethe say that conversation is the mode proper to the space before the door. So we stayed outside, moving outward from pedagogy as conversation's aspiration to the recognition of the unknowability of the Other as conversation's productive excess. Now we've stumbled into this *trap*—by way of Duchamp's found object of the same name—only to recognize in it a form isomorphic to the closed door from which we began. ("The trap," says Chow, "may therefore be analogized or approximated to a hinge or pivot, around which multiple planes rotate in perpetual slippage from one another, in such ways as to conjoin mobility with enclosure and alterity with capture."[47]) If the door, holding us in abeyance as its heralded Other, convoked all this discursive excess without our having even to move through or beyond it, it is hardly a stretch to say it thinks with an operational logic of the lure that cannot be dismissed.[48] The found-object door is a trap.

But we are not yet done. Step back again, this time to close in on things already familiar. The Australian anthropologist Deborah Bird Rose, writing about the technique of shimmer in Yolŋu art in a widely reviewed volume on aesthetics in ecocide (a volume that appears nearly a full decade after Lim herself first engaged shimmer), chooses and repeats a conspicuous word to describe the experience of the effect:

> When a painting reaches brilliance, for example, people say that it captures the eye much in the way the eye is captured by sun glinting on water. It is a capture that is all over the place: water capturing and reflecting the sun, the sun

> glinting on the water, the eyes of the beholders captured and enraptured, the ephemeral dance of it all. It is equally a lure: creatures long to be grabbed, to experience that beauty, that surprise, that gleaming ephemeral moment of capture.[49]

If it was implicit in Part I, here it is in full force: shimmer is a mechanism of entrapment or captivation in which the surfeit produced by the prey's necessary participation tips time and space into a plural and irreducible affective assemblage, "not you and me but something else still," as Ronell put it. Shimmer is what Whitten's *Door* effects, in its presentation of a surface as an intimation of depth; in its confusion of medium as both referent and substance; in its suspension of the viewer before it in simultaneous confusion, attraction, and participation. We cannot forgo the objects found within it *as external objects*, but neither can we reach them without obliterating their medium of presentation. Continually refusing to secure symbolic meaning, Whitten's *Door* keeps us forever on the doorstep: I cannot place either the function of paint or the status of the objects, and even when I see it, *I do not see what I am seeing*. Profounder still in Whitten's case is that this takes the color of a muted gray: shimmer is more than some extravagant colorist performance (as were Whitten's paintings from just before the fire, the ones like *Ascension I* (1979) he described as "the weaving of light"[50]); it is ontological, shimmer as a mode of being.

And here, one final backward step only to arrive again at the beginning. In Whitten's own words: "The painting as object *is skin and only skin*."[51]

Whatever happens, I want to *trap it in the surface*. I'm really into surface. [...] De Kooning said he wanted one skin [...]. *I want one skin too.*[52]

Shimmer is a matter of *surface*, all the way across.
Magic necessitates a new attitude to *skin*.
Conversation is a purchase on *alterity*.

And the appearance of an entryway comprised of found, symbolic things will always turn out to be only, in its surreptitious folding of material with perception, a gleaming *trap*.

(Exchange these terms at will.)

Without fail, every written account of *Extinction Events* obeys an implacable compulsion to recount the album's assemblage of found things, reconstructing verbatim from a list Lim herself first provided. We can give a brief recital of the listing here: (1) The very first sound heard, a trumpet and horn in fuzzy unison, is an elaborated transcription of the chromatic inner voices from "Naše večery," or "Our Evenings," the opening entry in Czech composer Leoš Janáček's piano cycle *On an Overgrown Path*; that trawling material will recursively form much of the work's harmonic structure; (2) following the interruption by the immense plastic sheet in the same track, there is a violin solo over which a small piccolo burst can be heard; that piccolo is a loose transcription of the 1987 last recording of Hawai'i's now-extinct Kauaʻi ʻōʻō bird; (3) in "Transmission," we have already said, lines of Lim's own violin solo *The Su Song Star Map* make up practice material for the duet; and (4) in "Dawn Chorus," the many handheld percussion instruments played by the ensemble recreate the revelatory 2016 recording of schools of singing sunrise fish off the coast of Australia's Port Hedland. Not to mention the literal found objects as well: in addition to the plastic sheet and the aluminum trays, we could also add the whirly tubes and PVC piping that in other places extend the musical landscape.

One can rather straightforwardly extrapolate the net of metaphors. The apparent randomness and diffusion of the musical objects mimic the ocean gyres—the systems of rotating currents—where plastic and natural organisms intermingle. But on closer inspection, they all cohere rather neatly: while the *musical* material from Janáček, for instance, permits a slippery harmonic field to lubricate elisions between disparate times and spaces, its *titles*, unspoken in the work but present as trace, neatly extend both the natural and solar themes of the work's speculative graft. (The latter thematic also taken up by the intertextual premise of *Su Song Star Map*.) The Kauaʻi ʻōʻō and fish chorus recordings, meanwhile, serve as inverse poles of the album's title. The bird is a present reverberation of a past small-scale extinction event (which in turn provides the haunting, negative face to the drum-violin dyad: where "Transmission" is the magic trick of a mute thing singing, the piccolo's Kauaʻi ʻōʻō call is the violent reanimation of what can no longer make noise [again, from Connor, on the double valence of ventriloquism in the nineteenth century: "Later in the century, ventriloquism, or the giving of voices to others, would be associated with the literal Frankenstein-like animation of the dead world of matter, in ways in which the giving of life is a murderous action"[53] {and indeed, there is something monstrous about this telephonic ensonging of the bird's dead corpse, not least about its necessity}].) The fish chorus, meanwhile, is the present speculation of a future aftermath of a global Extinction Event (the so-called "Sixth Mass Extinction": our own). This is a different sublime terror, that of having to imagine a song we will not hear. The instrumental extensions, meanwhile, keep a quantity of physical refuse circulating in the economy of the work.

But Lim's own reading on these objects troubles the apparent felicity of symbolic attributions. She ascribes them no stable status, describing the found objects instead as "fictional memory diagrams on which moments of incomplete recall and forgetting play out."[54] From the very first word we have a problem. The supposedly "real" things placed within an otherwise "invented" context are precisely those that she considers fictional. And here we come to the crux of the issue: like Whitten's *Door*, the status of these objects as *found* in *Extinction Events* is intensely troubled, even doubtful. One of the tenets—perhaps the only tenet—of Duchamp's readymades was the necessity of their recognizability as culturally ubiquitous. Readymades, he would say, are things at which you wouldn't otherwise look. *Trap* only works if an audience is capable of indexing the coatrack's certain existence elsewhere in identical and manufactured and *boring* form. Encountering it in the museum is an alienating surprise. What could possibly be the musical equivalent? What is the music you don't ordinarily even bother hearing whose garish unaltered infiltration of the work's acoustic place (but of course the infiltration is already an alteration: "anything at all, no matter how small or trivial—Duchamp's urinal—is transformed into a monument the moment it is placed in the museum with its identification tag"[55]) is precisely what makes it so scandalous? Impeding a satisfying answer is the fact that the ontological status of the object, so stable in visual art, is for music inherently diffuse and depropriative, hemorrhaging the boundaries between quotation, assemblage, found object, and pastiche. Said another way: readymade art works because something that should be *there* is *here* without giving up any of the attributes of *there*; music has a more difficult time keeping those things separate. Which is why the most literal presentations of found musical objects typically involve recordings played back during a live performance—the vinyl records played during Cage's *Europera 4*, for example—medial estrangement seemingly mandatory for the holding open of ontological difference. It is also why musical "found objects" veer towards canonized works, especially those percolating in the cultural milieu (think Mozart, Beethoven, *Carmina Burana*); these enjoy a secondary object-status separate from their ongoing existence as instantiated musical works that can be deployed as a signifier in place of the work itself. Else it is the index of genre that signs a musical alterity.

More often than not, however, at least New Musically speaking, "found musical objects"—which, let's clarify, should not be confused with "found instruments"—involve preexisting sonic material whose original state provides the impetus for an infective or pathogenic composing-in.[m] Sometimes they are announced; sometimes they go unmentioned; sometimes they're recognizable; sometimes they're hidden. But the stark divergences in status of the found object—Duchamp uses mass-manufactured commodities, Lim is using natural artifacts

[m] One thinks of Ming Tsao's interventions into Schoenberg and Zumsteeg, or the entire project of Michael Finnissy.

and other art—and the differentials of medial incorporation—music is hard-pressed to achieve art's index of exteriority—compromise music's capacity to enact precisely the same undermining of the authority-status of art. Not to mention she infects them, alters them, makes them her own. If these are found objects, they are failed or insufficient ones.

What I am getting at is the *why* and the *what* of Lim's collection of musical found objects. Their nonabsorption in the body of the work is crucial to *Extinction Events* thematic project (plastic is a foreign substance caught in oceanic time), but their perceptual obscurity renders them unrecognizable—and so ineffective—without a map. What I am asking about is their being found objects (and that's precisely the term she uses for them in her essay on *Extinction Events*) at all. What is this necessity of *having been told they're there*, or, more to the point, *having been told they exteriorize and precede this work*? Even the most specialized of listener, a trained ornithologist or a Janáček expert, would fail to recognize these externalities, so mutated and obscured are their re-presentations. And yet she gives them to us as worthy of note, with the natural implication that they are intended to be recognized.

That is the implication. But the reality is, I think, just the reverse. By my measure, these found objects, insofar as they are in the piece, are there for the sole purpose of *being given to us*; or, rather, their presence facilitates a performance of the gesture of informational provisions so as to draw scrutiny to data's interpretive portability. As in Whitten, Lim's found objects simulate the gesture or shape of a doorway, a means of getting into the piece. (Which is why reviewers so often reprint them: they mistake information as an entryway, failing to notice that one cannot actually pass into the work's meaningful depths through them.) If they turn up as imperfectly, insufficiently, or unsatisfactorily presented in the music, it is in the interest of keeping us in Goethe's anteroom where ethical relations to Art and Nature are still possible. Knowledge does not give a guarantee. Getting through the door, getting "inside the piece," breaking it apart, unscrambling its logic, hunting down its every corner—these colonial impulses offer no rewards here. (I admitted up front that all promises and returns are off; I meant it.)

And here the shimmer's relay once more beginning: the purported existence of these objects elsewhere sends the album's curious listener on a hunt for the originals which, once found, only necessitate a return to the album to verify just how true a transcription was made. Listening afresh to the original, the supposedly primed attendee recognizes: the two don't sound the same. Or, better, if the opening smear sounds anything like Janáček, it was only our attention that put him there. Back and forth, back and forth, we reconstruct the aura of the living thing by our own libidinal investment, one the music itself fails to summon. This is what Lim meant when she called them "fictional memory diagrams on which moments of incomplete recall and forgetting play out": what they index is not the presence of an absolute outside but that (a) there is no secure conceptual outside in the age of entangled meltdown, and (b) mastery of depth is a fictional endeavor that only rebounds you to the surface. Scratch away at Whitten's cassette tape or his fish; arrive only at more paint. Lim's found objects perform the insufficiency of every promise of information as the mastery of music.[n] They are a trap we're

[n] Which is, in some sense, what a book series like this appears to promise as well.

meant to fall for, making us the prey: by Chow's scheme, then, shimmer and song would be the supplementary excess from within us rupturing the discursive unity of "the work."

Earlier we listed the four sonic "objects" floating around in *Extinction Events*. I want us to addend an unlicensed fifth. The title of the second track—"Retrograde Inversion"—is a nod to an insider-baseball-type compositional technique from way back in New Music's founding days, in which earlier material was mapped upside-down and backward to generate new fields of music. Its appearance here is both a literal index of method—the pitches in track two are, in fact, largely pilfered from material originally presented in track one, albeit rendered virtually unrecognizable after extreme transformation—and a conceptual overtone, suggesting the weird compressions and violent upturns of material in the age of meltdown: everything is *topsy-turvy*. If, however, we take retrograde to also mean its more colloquial abbreviation "retro," the title might also be read literally as "Old-Fashioned Inversion," or, even more generally, "Out-of-Date Technique." However we read it, the title signals the track as somehow bound to a heyday of its own artistic movement, the presence of which here suggests—as, in a more contained sense, does the appearance of Lim's violin solo in track four—that the history of New Music itself is one object among many swept away in the gyres of ecocide.

But push this further: to subtitle an entire passage of a work "Retrograde Inversion" plays on an entrenched New Music tendency to overinvest in the identification of compositional technique as productive interpretation. Lim goes ahead and tells us up front precisely how this music got made and exactly where to look, both inviting the inevitable army of tweed theorists who will go hunting for the proof while dissuading their satisfaction by giving the game away up front. The fake-out—the *trap*, we might say—is that a more extensive knowledge of the compositional *how* here does nothing to heighten an experience of the *what*. Lim's tongue-in-cheek subtitle can be read as another *mise en abyme*. Just as the literal door of Whitten's painting is both the figure into which found objects adhere *and* a found object in its own right, Lim's imputation of compositional technique as just another piece of data whose discovery effects no satisfying end undoes the predicate of mastery on which the field has, until now, attempted to measure proficiency. She sets a trap for a field she knows will try to exercise mastery at any turn possible, forcing it to concede its own methodology and confront its entanglement in the production of a surface. This is the pedagogy of which we spoke earlier: Lim is rehearsing how we will rewrite our terms of engagement with music for a more ethical imagining at the end of the world by tripping up, like Duchamp's *Trap*, all the old terms.

Push it further still: the associations of "Retrograde Inversion" redouble with significance in the context of climate meltdown and re-enchantment. A foundational mechanism of dodecaphonic logic, the name harkens inexorably to the early days of New Music's disenchanting of nature, that Second Viennese School serialization of parameters later epitomized by Stockhausen. It drags in by the ear a time when the old magic of music's relationship to nature was under extreme Enlightenment duress, just as the invocation of "found objects" calls to a similarly singular moment of upheaval in art history. (Both Duchamp's *Fountain* and Arnold Schoenberg's first application of total serial logic appear within five years of each other.) For her part, Lim has recommended the Janáček to similar effect: its inclusion is "a way of invoking a certain liminal corner of musico-historical time and place, straddling a passage from the nineteenth century into the twentieth with a music infused with longing for a world that can no longer be recuperated."[56] But the cases bear an important difference. The Czech citation carries an imagined heredity, a kind of transhistoric sympathy or kinship Lim feels with Janáček and his ethnographic moment. "Retrograde Inversion" is less affective; no, stronger, it is *the very treatment of musical material as sequences of data absent any affect*. The historicity of an impulsive will to knowledge becomes, in the final analysis, just another fictional object on which to exercise some forgetting, a mere "trace of a trace of something long extinguished."[57]

One can imagine a lesser version of *Extinction Events* in which all found objects are preserved in their original state, electronically reproduced (a piano sample of Janáček, an audio file of the fish) to literalize—or at least more accurately simulate—the trash islands of oceanic gyres. If this imagined version is pallid and impoverished, it has to do with music's unique capacity for mimesis. New Music has a colloquial saying that certain musics "teach you how to listen to them." In her forgetting, overwriting, suppressing, destroying, and redirecting of attention and material away from certainty and toward the libidinal investments in shimmer's excesses, Lim is exercising what Taussig called *knowing what not to know*, getting us practiced in the affective emissions—confusion, bafflement, perhaps even disappointment!—of a masterful knowledge coming up short in the age of re-enchantment.

We are continually compelled back to skin. (This is, after all, what shimmer does.)

Jack Whitten chose his words carefully. Calling the technique that made *Door to Manhattan* a skin rendered it nothing but exteriority, nothing but surface, which is also to say—if we were less generous—lacking depth, lacking substance even; why would one spend time with something so self-avowedly superficial? And yet, as Connor points out in his *Book of Skin*, it is precisely in the nature of a surface to be inscribed upon:

> The skin figures. It is what we see and know of others and ourselves. We show ourselves in and on our skins, and our skins figure out the things we are and mean: our health, youth, beauty, power, enjoyment, fear, fatigue, embarrassment or suffering. The skin is always written: it is legendary.[58]

Whitten himself saw that connection: "Skin is the largest organ of the body. Skin is also the catalyst of race in America. My paint is my skin. Paint as skin is the foundation of my process. My 'processes' are all about skin."[59] Skin is always inscribed, "written," Connor says. Which is also to suggest it is in the nature of a skin to be *read*.

When the philosopher Jean-Luc Nancy, at the end of his life, wrote a book about humanity's destruction of the planet, he called it *The Fragile Skin of the World*. His wager—and it runs counter to much of ecological thought—was on figuring the world as a series of pressures and impressions, inscriptions and incisions upon the collective skin of mankind. It was the great philosopher of touch's dying wish that we not forget skin-to-skin contact as the site where ethical alterity is highest, the touch of skin as where I become most certain *I am not you*. I cannot enter. I am always in the entryway of your skin, that antechamber where Goethe said ethical relations to Nature and Art began.

> The skin is not the site of circulation and measurement: it is a place of passage, of transit and transport, of traffic and transaction. It is a place where rubbing and irritation, mingling and distinguishing, and colliding and stroking all take place. The skin is erectile, bristling, quivering, retractile, caressing, lubricating, squeezing, trembling. [...] In every way, the skin translates, betrays, transpires, and transudes *the palpitating singularity of the enigma of a being-to-itself that is thoroughly outside of itself, near and distant, multiple* [...]. In every way, it is the powerful and fragile resonance of everything that brings about a form or a tone of existence.[60]

Liza Lim set out to trace ecocide's injunction to imagination and thought. If she produced a work of skin, it is because the touching of a surface without passing through it is an acknowledgment of where this body ends and another one begins. It is to accede to the limited contingency of encounter, to recognize the self as touched in the instant that it touches. Skin enfolds difference without subtracting it. Lim's music touches things without consuming them whole, allowing them to inscribe upon its surface without demanding their complete agglutination: "the powerful and fragile *resonance* of everything." Our attention is one of these things it touches, one of the things from which it beckons the inscription of a resonance. So is history. So is nature. So is the entire field of practice into which she deposits its abyssal work. *Extinction Events* is skin-deep, because that is where everything touches everything.

p.s., or, a skin graft

Not for nothing too might we notice that Connor, Whitten, and Nancy all perform the traditional style of skin-writing, those long phrases accruing powers, adjectives, and ascriptions that on their own would unsatisfactorily account for the subject at hand. Plurality, a recitation of multiplicity, is how skin speaks (commas, after all, being the linguistic production of touch). "Endless Andness" is what Mieke Bal calls a mist or a fog that spreads out to touch everything to itself.[61] All those terms hinging together, pivoting on the comma, multiple planes rotating in perpetual slippage from one another. "[Skin] is, and it is nothing but, the whole of the combinations [...], their folds ..."[62]

—(and then remember that the mimetic impulse to write objects in a row as some kind of shibboleth is precisely the aperture through which *Extinction Events* compels its own coming into language. Even in our failing, it speaks through us to attest to the inarticulable condition of its being.)

A FOLD or A CONTINGENCY or AN ORNAMENT

"I'll be this skin tomorrow.

[...]

"I'll be this skin tomorrow.

"And as I anoint her I cultivate time with both hands, one on top of the other hers yours mine ours, I spread them, I feel them, I browse and I ruminate the future. I study: the way death lets us feel its delicate, intricate bites. How it is already here a little, nibbling. Its inroads. How life gives them back. How it gets its strength and body back by stirring up, citing, resuscitating along the paths of dreams.

"And it is during these times, when *all is lost* that I finally come up with the answer to death, the road to happiness *through* pain: this is something-other-than a dream, this is the hyperdream."[63]

Interstice: In

(among the pleats of matter)

> *Stay at the skin, don't move on, find where it ruptures, fold-catastrophe, bring it through to the ceiling, continue to infinity.*

In 2022, Lim followed up *Extinction Events* with a second Kairos portrait album° called *Annunciation Triptych*. Cast in three tracks for orchestra, that album covers some familiar territory: ecology, feminist reclamation, states of ecstasy, drums that sing. Donna Haraway's beloved Hawai'ian bobtail squid even gets an honorable mention. But smack in the middle of the middle track is a blinding moment of musical force that Seth Brodsky mused was "one of the strangest moments [. . .] in Lim's entire body of work."[64] He describes it: "A cadenza for horns, percussion, and piano winnows to a single bass string played inside the piano's body, generating higher and higher partials. Then silence. Then BOOM, an enormous chord from the orchestra." That BOOM, the sudden irruption of orchestral power, is cataclysmic to the album, a rift that, once torn, refuses all attempts to think the album whole. The BOOM, in other words, cannot be taken back. Brodsky, hearing backward, likens it to a displaced Extinction Event, "one moment," he says, "*where the world actually ends*."[65]

At first glance, Brodsky's nod to *Extinction Events* appears to invoke the earlier work as a *category* of Lim's thought, a conceptual habitus of her work to simulate eschatology

---

° New Music's recording industry frequently prioritizes CDs devoted to the work of a single composer, preferring their facilitation of multifaceted "portrait" of the artist. Kairos was, at one time, the standard-bearer for such albums.

so as to practice how we think through what comes after. But taking his suggestion literally, we find a very particular node of connection. In *Annunciation Triptych*, the chords—BOOM!—are a catastrophe of form. They are like nothing that came before, an utterance the nature and violence of which—an eviscerating reintroduction of explicit tonality, a half-diminished chord resolving to B major bright with brass and string—forces the listener to rethink the very capacity and enunciative place of the work. The chords, placed in so foreign a context, appear like a nineteenth-century quotation. (They appear, at first glance, like a *found object*!) That they are not undoes all expectations about how the work listens to itself, and how it should be listened to in turn: *If this was possible, what does that do to everything that came before?*[p]

By Lim's own attestation, *Extinction Events* is a work about plastic: its circulation, its half-life, its particulate infection of breathing bodies, and its ghostly tendency to linger. Plastic is a stylus for tracing oceanic movements that buffet and grind it; it is, however, only sparingly literal. But in the very first track, a *mise en abyme* opens up as plastic rises out of its metaphoric function to interrupt and in some senses *destroy* the boundaries between concept and material on which the work has so far hung its hat. It is this interruption—the enormous sheet of paper-thin plastic whose extended haptic rustling stops the music in its tracks and forces a reconceptualization of the scope and apparatus of the work—that constitutes, by my measure, the formal BOOM!, the Extinction Event of *Extinction Events*.

---

p One could think of the tonal emergences in "Autocorrect" on similar, though not identical, lines.

When the work is played live, the violinist conveys the unwieldy sheet as a long, slow procession from the back to the front of the concert hall, alternatively wearing and activating its noisy folds. They mount the stage, whereupon the sheet gets passed hand to hand over the heads of the ensemble until it reaches the percussionist, who bundles it up and continues to make noise as the violinist picks up their instrument and begins to play. A sonic continuity is thus drawn between the literal refuse and the music, a spectrum of shimmer. When done live, the source of the interruption is easily clarified, with location as the index of exteriority: the sound comes from the back of the hall, not the front where the rest of the performers are; the piece "stops," drawing attention to the acoustic non-belonging of a plastic event so as to demonstrate its reabsorption into the interior of the work.[q] On the album, the effect is much more hallucinogenic: it is as if playback itself has gone haywire with telephonic presences, plastic metempsychosing into a staticky, speaking ghost in the machine.

There is much discussion in eco-criticism about the consequences of what is referred to as the global economy's *plastic turn*;[66] this interstice turns turnings into *folds*. Taking Lim's sheet literally as a creased, pleated matter that

---

[q] One recalls the tactic by groups like Extinction Rebellion, popularized in the late 2010s and mobilized by social media attention, of interrupting symphony concerts as a means of drawing bourgeois attention to ecocide. In Lim's iteration, it is no longer the people in opposition to global warming but *the plastic itself*, loosed and magnified as both within (microplastics) and without (disrupting), that brings the music to a halt. Here, the transporting human says nothing at all, a mute vessel for this impossibly noisy and distracting object.

unsettles by infinitely converging all notions of inside and outside, this distinctly catastrophic *mise en abyme* bespeaks a Baroque metaphysics proper. Gilles Deleuze's defining trait of Baroque expression is a correspondence between what he calls *the pleats of matter* and *the folds of the soul*, a kind of inextricability between subject and object, representation and perception that is distinctly, well, *plastic*: the fold folds. Among the six defining traits of the Baroque, Deleuze will name three that are already intimately familiar here: *the fold*, *the inside and the outside*, and *texture*.[67] But he will also routinely name song as the mysterious product par excellence of the movement between matter and soul: "The fold is divided into folds, which are tucked inside and which spill onto the outside [...]. Pleats of matter in a condition of exteriority, folds of the soul in a condition of closure. Pleats of the partition and folds of the song."[68]

It hardly needs being said that the continuous rustling of the thin sheet makes an adjectivally *shimmering* sound. But, more to the point, the plastic acts like a conceptual vortex, at once literal matter and symbolic designate. Belonging both to the absolute interior of *Extinction Events*—plastic as disruptive material force—and to its absolute exterior in its shattering of the very limits of the performance space, plastic is a territorializing force that is always already at home. "As a general rule," Deleuze says, "the way a material is folded is what constitutes its texture. It is defined less by its heterogeneous and really distinct parts than by the style by which they become inseparable by virtue of particular folds."[69] The auditory texture of *Extinction Events* as an event of absolute surface, we have already said, can be read on that continuous spectrum of shimmer: here we understand why. Perception and object fold over at the edges, creating an inseparability that generates endless dilation and hallucinatory blur.

But we are not done following it through to infinity just yet. The violin, we have already said, has to pick up and play while the plastic keeps sounding, establishing a telephonic connection between the two. But, like any fold, this local and literal hinge has a global, conceptual counterpart. In what is a radical departure from tradition and a startlingly original reimagining of fundamental musical notations, Lim unbinds the sovereignty of linear time across *Extinction Events* through a net of cross-hatched repeat signs that send whole phrases crashing back in spirals upon themselves. We can see this—with an added diagrammatic tracing—in the violin's final bar of "Transmission": beginning at the star, the player spins out a long helix of smaller returns that rupture from within any gestural cohesion of the musical material (Figure 3). The figure is both utterly destabilized, never heard in its "complete" form, and paradoxically reinstalled as vaster and more thorough than itself. Indeed, the very premise of an infinite but discontinuous net of repetitions recalls the "infinity of 'little convex mirrors'" Deleuze noticed when he saw his own image enlarged and deformed in Caravaggio's white paints.[70] Elsewhere, describing

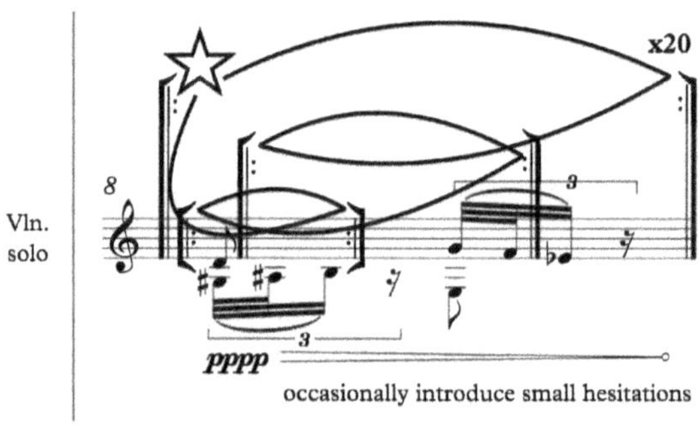

Figure 3 *Liza Lim, "Transmission," from* Extinction Events and Dawn Chorus, *bar 8. Used with permission.*

the nested mirrors of folds, he writes: "the parts of matter form little vortices in a maelstrom, and in those are found even more vortices, even smaller, and even more are spinning in the concave intervals of the whirls that touch one another."[71] The nouns here—vortexes, maelstroms, whirls—are conspicuously apt: Lim conceived of the repeat structures as a mimetic approximation of the violent oceanic currents that break up plastic matter into microscopic particles while simultaneously banding trash together into monstrous conglomerates: the fold "flips from large to minuscule and back again," the smallest unit that contains infinity.[72]

But it is still only a mimetic likeness, and here the mastery of non-mastery returns with force. Lim's notation is, as we can see above, neither prescriptive nor absolute: there is no definitive "map" through which to read the epicycles (the above is just one rendering). Slippage and loss are endemic to nested repeats, and their potentially infinite nature requires every player to craft personal solutions for both getting caught and, eventually, getting out. Time and material thus become impossibly tangled with subjectivity and memory. Unlike strict iteration, the player cannot simply lull into perfect similitude. These require active, constant upkeep and attention—but that's not to say one cannot certainly get *lost* in the folds. Perhaps, after the fifteenth cycle, the violinist jumps back one too far or forgets where a particular repeat ends, causing the listener to hear echoes of things that either haven't happened, or didn't happen, or simply don't exist. The whole does not exist except as a virtual coordination between listener and music, a mirage of familiarity: we *hear what we never hear*. It is this continuous loss by continuous return—this "haze of dust without objects that the figures themselves raise up from the depths, and that falls back again, but with time enough to be seen for an instant"[73]—that creates what Deleuze calls the *hallucinatory perception* of the Baroque fold:

> Minuscule folds that are endlessly unfurling and bending on the edges of juxtaposed areas, like a mist or fog that makes their surface sparkle [we might say *shimmer*], at speeds that no one of our thresholds of consciousness could sustain in a normal state.[74]

And indeed, the threshold (doorway!) of consciousness is where we permanently are. The crisis of ecocide is a frightening imbrication of outside with inside, subject with object. There is no longer an "outside" from which to assess climate warming: we are all *in it*. And it is *in us* in turn, microplastics swimming in the brains and bloods of those bodies trying to hold it as an object just long enough to think it seriously. Lim regularly cites Chris Jordan's famous photos of the albatross corpses from Midway Atoll as a primary influence on *Extinction Events*, the devastating violence of an outside too much on the inside (Figure 4). The emotional valence of the photo is tripled when we realize that our corpses will all look much the same. Paintings of mixed objects were at one time called *still lifes*, that is to say *dead*. Folds inside of folds.

The art historian Mieke Bal has worked extensively on the burbling quotations of Baroque techniques in twenty-first-century art. Her thesis—and I think it's a good one—is that citational practices do more than quote: they actively rewrite the history they cite. Like Lim's entangled revisioning of the early twentieth-century avant-garde as a kind of portal within her work, Bal likewise postulates a thread of bidirectional exchange between the Baroque and Modernity. Here she is rehashing Deleuze on the Baroque, but just as easily describing the experience of *Extinction Events*:

Figure 4 *Chris Jordan, "Unaltered stomach contents of a Laysan albatross fledgling," Midway Island, 2009. Public domain.*

> There is no longer any telling apart the historically remote object and the historically near subject of interpretation, for the subject in turn has become an object of interpolation, and henceforward these positions of object and subject have become caught in the movement that inscribed the act of viewing in time, while at the same time being fundamentally unstoppable.[75]

Liza Lim, it has not been said enough—with her mirroring distortions, her ornamented time, her chiaroscuro textures, her extreme correlativism of subject and object, her obsession with skin and surface, her folding histories, her hallucinatory vertigo—is history's most Baroque composer.

A TRICK or A CONVERSATION or A HALLUCINATION

"Docile I say not a word the dream dictates I obey eyes closed. I have learned this docility. The dream commands. I do."[76]

Part III: Dream

(a fiction)

The shaman and his patient cut a curious dance. Sitting astride the social order, they are, by their lonesome, figures of failed integration, "the patient, because he is ill, and the sorcerer, because he is neurotic."[77] Claude Lévi-Strauss is blunt. Sickness compromises the stable subject, exposing the body to a problem the mind cannot rationalize away, inexpressibility and absent origins all upsetting the order of things known. Shamanism, meanwhile, is structural excess, "overflow[ing] with emotional interpretations and overtone, in order to supplement an otherwise deficient reality."[78] Shaman and patient are thus mutually dependent aberrations, each requiring the other for purchase of their entry ticket to the fairground of community. Together, they (re)perform the making-sense of the insensible for the edification of the community, retuning their truths to the worlds these performances think up. Shamanism requires an audience, who in turn require shamanism. Lévi-Strauss called this "fireworks."[79]

There is a good case to be made that we are all of us sick these days, in some way or another. Nietzsche called man "the most imperiled, the most chronically and profoundly sick of all sick animals,"[80] and that was before microplastics and ozone and GMOs and brainrot and … and … and. When Paul Preciado named modern capitalism a *pharmacopornographic* regime, he was emphasizing the extent to which sickness and its prolonged endurance have become entangled in bare living.[81] Notice, too, the *graphic* suffix, writing always furnishing the site where the erotic and the indisposed meet in their hallucinogenic and unproductive surfeit. This is what Avital Ronell meant when she suggested that the War on Drugs was a war on literature as much as on addiction.[82] To talk of sickness and magic healing is to talk of junkies and scribblers: a quartet fallen out of normative psychic economies. These days, everyone is an amateur junkie, all benzodiazepines and THC and adderall. But these are only pharmaceutically induced suppressions, nothing magic about them. We know well the sick and the drugged; the writers and the shamans are less certain. And while there is, indeed, magic in this re-enchanted world—we've chased song, magic, tricks, traps, shimmers, folds, and ventriloquisms of several kinds, a veritable lexicon of shamanic effects—we have not yet stopped to ask: for whom and by whom are there spells?

It would be easy, of course, to invoke the *composer-as-magician* trope, rerouting *what the sorcerer said* back into the author's voice.[83] Easy, likewise, to say the composer performs *the skilled revelation of skilled concealment* in her acoustic trickery and get on with things.[r] The formula "*Extinction Events is a spell woven by the shaman Liza Lim to heal our ecological sickness*" looks nice on paper. Shamans, after all, frequently sing. And the formula performs well: as recently as July of 2025, a marketing campaign for her portrait concert at the Zagreb Biennale emphasized "shamanism and magic" and "rituals and life transitions" as major themes of Lim's work. But I'm not so sure the circuit is that simple. Off the bat, the equation of shamanism with art-making is, as Taussig was at pains to point out, already a colonial move to invest Western poiesis with Indigenous magical powers. By Taussig's measure, true shamanism looks much more like "an artisan facing a down-to-earth problem to be worked at with the diligence of a craft."[84]

---

r The title of Jessie Fillerup's recent study of Ravel, *Magician of Sound*, says it all.

Which is not yet to exclude composition from shamanic practice (on the contrary: composition is colloquially called a "craft"). But we should remain wary of ulterior motivations for dressing the composer in magician's robes. After all, calling something magic always retroactively affirms the absolute of God and science by depositing a key structural difference: magic is always the incomprehensible practice of the Other. If the composer is a shaman, there remains a mystic alterity about what she does, thus permitting the holding of her work in permanent abeyance from rigorous and nonsymbolic meaning. If the composer is a shaman, criticism is never obligated to engage her on any terms beyond the pleasure of wide-eyed wonder. Nietzsche himself knew this when, sick with diphtheria from the Prussian front, he initially sought out Wagner to furnish the means of his recovery. Only later would he break from what he called Wagner's *spell*, comparing the old composer to both Circe and Klingsor, dark magicians who wielded their power of sensuality over and against freedom, "a profile of sickness that permits no further doubt"; *not-thinking* is one consequence of being taken in by composerly magic.[85]

Lim has—like Nietzsche, who rejected it in Wagner—already dismissed attempts to modulate her music into redemptive or *healing* functions: we saw this in the Introduction. Accordingly, one cannot take stock of the meaning-making apparatus of *Extinction Events* without confronting an ending in which humanity does not figure. "Dawn Chorus" is Marlene Dietrich crooning over the closing shots of animal and apian ongoingness at the hour of mass human death in Yorgos Lanthimos's *Bugonia*: "Where have all the graveyards gone? Gone to flower, every one!" except in Lim the song's imperative refrain—"When will they ever learn?"—goes missing. *Extinction Events* neither *resolves* nor *demands otherwise.* But then neither does one write a work like *Extinction Events* without experiencing at least some ethical imperative to intervene in the fields of behavior, concept, and idea (or, rather, to trace Gaia's intrusion on that most human domain of art so as to call attention to her catastrophic unsettling of all three). In other words, there is at least *some* relation between the album and our present ways of being in and with climate change that necessitates a mapping. It just cannot be inflected into positivism, and it certainly does not meet the criteria for a palliative.

Let's look again at the terrain to be mapped. Global warming is the paradigmatic hyperobject in Timothy Morton's account: too big to feel, too vast to know, troubling our access to concepts and symbols by availing us only in fragmentary experiences that never reveal the whole.[86] Global warming, it has been continuously said, is a crisis of *thought*, and while there are indeed physical sicknesses associated with it—famine, weather-related injury, the spread of mass disease, respiratory fatigue—their care and comprehension is impeded by what are primarily psychological symptoms: mental roadblocks, imaginative shortcomings, futility hedged at every turn by an incapacity to conceive at scale our place in the Anthropocene.[5] If there is a sickness to which *Extinction Events* bears relation, it is a philosophical one that supersedes the atomized body. Other albums of magic medicine for late capitalism—Esperanza Spalding's *Twelve Little Spells*, for example—target various appendages and fleshy regions of the individual. *Extinction Events* rushes straight to the collective head.

---

[5] A World Health Organization bulletin on climate change lists "immediate mental health issues" first on the summary of induced sicknesses, followed only then by long-term illness.[87]

Now go over the shaman-patient-audience triad once more, for the pathways of exchange are not as hammered or one-directional as their colonially cast roles might otherwise have it. Lévi-Strauss, comparing shamanism to psychoanalysis,[t] proposed that every performance "always involves the shaman's enactment of the 'call,' or the initial crisis which brought him the revelation of his condition."[88] The shaman is thus an exceptional abreactor in that old psychoanalytic sense, reliving his own "original trauma" so as to model and encourage new treatment. And that traumatic "call" to shamanism is always a *skepticism*, a profound doubt that the call comes at all. Taussig relays the story of Santiago Mutumbajoy, a shaman who witnessed colonial medicine heal his wife when so many Indigenous shamans could not. "All those shamans had been fakes," Taussig says, "and at that moment he decided to be a shaman."[89] The magician thus "becomes [. . .] a famous shaman not so much despite but *because of his profoundly skeptical attitude*."[90] There is in all magic this ontic aporia, a sickness of the healer whose doubtful distrust of magic paradoxically installs the necessary conditions for the patient's belief and the magic's success.

This immediately cross-checks any impulse we might harbor to metamorphose the composer into a healing magician. To the contrary, one of the defining characteristics of composer behavior is a near-delusional *belief* in one's own music: it is a vital shield against the onslaught of accusations of elitism, obsolescence, and cultural irrelevance. If there is magic in sound, composers are the most prone to believing in it. The

[t] In what turned out to be a misguided move, he overinvested in magic as a product of intelligence, leaving the mimetic body by the wayside.

shaman is not so easily swept up. Perhaps, then, we should think about where magic meets the patient, an exercise for which Taussig, in his revisions of Lévi-Strauss, will be most useful. Taussig ascribes considerable capaciousness to the shaman-patient dyad, redirecting some interpretive functionality back to the patient, who in Lévi-Strauss's account remains essentially mute: "the power of shamanism lies not with the shaman but with the differences created by the coming together of shaman and patient," goes Taussig's thesis.[91] He reads doubt and confidence, healing and illness, interpretation and craft as essentially enantiodromic: the shaman projects confidence because she is the original doubter, while the patient, plagued by epistemic doubt and hovering on the "hermeneutic brink,"[92] knits new personal significance through the shaman's practiced moves. It is the patient who provides the terms of magic's future integration with the social fabric and who, after she is cured, becomes its affirmative mouthpiece. The shaman merely invokes the conditions necessary for animating and (in a very Haraway-inflected posthuman sense) agentizing sickness as a discursive, thinking partner, even friend. At core, however, Taussig reads shaman and patient as emanating from a single point:

> Both figures, that of the shaman as certainty and that of patient as doubt, only acquire this configuration by their coming together, because both contain within themselves, taken as individuals, *the same vexation* with regard to the credible impossibilities that course though life's contingencies as much as through the ambiguities of social relations. The creative delicacy of their coming together as patient and shaman lies in the different yet complementary ways this relation allows them to ease or resolve this vexation. [...] Each person here provides the other with a special

> viewpoint and function in *the making and always provisional interpretation* of society's imaginative infrastructure.[93]

If pressed, then, I would contend that Lim is indeed *not* the shaman producing bundles of extra meaning to reconcile our cognitive sickness with some "healthier" society (not least because, in the age of meltdown, who among us would constitute the "healthy"?). For my money, this music is—and I know it will come across as scandalous; the move is calculated—*the illness itself*. It is the mastery of non-mastery of the psychic pathogenicity of meltdown, a mimetic redoubling of its agential thinking. Now there is, of course, a long and troubled social history of composition as psychic sickness (the hearing of invisible music always a near-indicator of schizophrenia). But I want to resist ascribing music as a *sickness-of*, reinstalling a human vector whose subjective experience would cordon illness into a merely symbolic meaning. We have continued to say that the posthuman bent of *Extinction Events* obliges us to think expressive agency beyond the human: that obligation in turn demands we decouple sickness from any signifying body. Liza Lim, then, is one of the *sick* in this advanced climate catastrophe. But the sickness that is *Extinction Events*, this *expressive thought of cognitive sickness under global warming*, does not belong to her and is not *of* her. Nor is it a mere representation, a simulacrum of how cognitive sickness *feels*. Like the shaman whose invocation to illness as a partner in the dance creates the conditions for creative and flexible responses to and with it, it is in our interest to think illness as an agent, with all the aesthetic and cognitive autonomy that implies. (Not least because the imaginative roadblocks induced by climate crisis then go from an "*I* can't" to "something in our way," the latter infinitely more navigable and receptive to change. Enlightenment would no longer be an innate and immobile condition of existence but a territorializing pathogen, and so one still capable of engagement.)

Staying with music and illness a little longer, one finds the negative parallel—that is, the music with bacteria-resistant humanism intact—in Mozart's *Die Zauberflöte* (*The Magic Flute*). In Part I, we traced the mimetic Enlightenment echo by which New Music restaged the alienation of nature and song. If *Extinction Events* is the categorical rejection of those neo-Enlightenment values through the lending of song to sickness, *Zauberflöte* is immunization against infection as the installation of Enlightenment itself.[u] One can see this in Ronell's reading of the Queen of the Night as "Mozart's great antibody" whose gift of immunity to Tamino—the magic flute, what Ronell calls the "stylus of immunization" or simply "health"—will ultimately render her inoperant when her immunodeficiency is coopted and incorporated by Sarastro's Enlightenment regime.[94] The opera, by Ronell's measure, plays out along a discourse of immunology: "A passive, maternal immunity [is] granted to an exogenous invader who will in turn prove injurious to the noble host, nurse, and nourisher, perhaps, indeed, causing infection more by exploiting host susceptibility than by its own powers of pathogenicity. For they are weak, they are wretched and wretching; they need help, the strong."[95] Health is the Mozartean index of Enlightenment ascension, castrating nature in its pharmaceutical immunocompetence.

Virginia Woolf, lying feverish in bed, reads poetry with revelatory attendance to the texture of language, forgetting,

---

[u] A citation made doubly apt when one remembers that the human-bird hybrid is a figure common to both: Papageno appears in clarinet form in Lim's *Tree of Codes*, premiered the year before *Extinction Events*.

as if for the first time, to read for meaning. "In health meaning has encroached upon sound,"[96] she complains. If Woolf is right, it is a particular trait of the healthy to entreat the well-behaved symbolic. Health is immunization from sound as sound, and there is something accordingly *sick* about hearing music without making the symbolic modulation. Like Ronell's Sarastro and the character she puns as "Contamino," the immunocompetent are wretched and dangerous for their health, while the immunocompromised and sick emerge as Nietzsche's truth-tellers. So long as *illness* is, *qua* Sontag, retained *as metaphor*, it remains unassimilated and threatening: it is only by relinquishing conceptual *control* on illness, by refusing to treat the pen as a stylus of immunity, that we can draw into the ring the thinking habitus of the underside of Enlightenment objectivity and learn to think with, rather than about (which is to say against) it. Health: what got us into this mess; sickness: how we might get out.

Music, when it is art, exposes and holds open—like illness in Lévi-Strauss's account—the unthought and unthinkable of a society. If *Extinction Events* is so moving, it is precisely because its dual citizenship as art and illness holds it in the anteroom of established economies of meaning. The shaman for this musical sickness, then, would be the writer, the neurotic called upon to render for an audience those unthinkables as integrable again, even if it means revisioning the truths of being, imagining, and organizing to which the audience ascribes. In Stanley Cavell's well-mannered account of the task of music criticism—"the opening of access between the artist and his audience, giving voice to the legitimate claims of both"[97]—one can already hear an acute preview of what Taussig later described as the shaman-patient's "making and always provisional interpretation of society's imaginative infrastructure." Contingent, emergent, and ongoing, the work of the writer-shaman is not in empirical diagnostics but rather in a continuous creative scaffolding of the hole-riddled landscape of the collective imaginary. Not to mention that writing, like shamanism, is a practical craft whose mastery of non-mastery ("the category of saying-more-than-we-know-we-are-saying," Hélène Cixous says[98]) generates a semiotic excess colloquially called "poetry" but more often experienced as *magic*.

The password hinging *writer* to Lévi-Strauss and Taussig's *shaman* is, by my measure, that abreactive *call*. With each new performance, the shaman relives the *call*, which, we've already said, entails an absolute doubt and skepticism about shamanic epistemology. Is not the writer that same practical skeptic, the one who refuses to take as given all those claims about musical significance and affective thrust? Likely the writer is one who has been duped (or, better yet, *failed* to be duped) by music-critical prose before and so takes up the pen with intent to unmask the trickster-writer as a fraud. In doing so, she becomes a rather adroit magician of her own, her writing born of a vivified skepticism that pushes up against programs of sedimented interpretation. All those sicknesses, those gaps where thought comes up short and for which others have failed to account, become, for her, privileged interlocutors against which to make her provisional interpretations. Jean-Luc Nancy formulated this paradoxical folding nature of the music-writer's abreaction: "Something attracts us and *calls us* beyond the simple act of listening. But this 'beyond' happens in the listening."[99] In other words, this practical skeptic of the efficacy of words is called to write not by literature itself but by some unidentifiable, inexplicable dimension accessible only in the instant of perception and for which all words have formerly failed to account. One is called because words have failed to name what listening hears. (Think of all those inadequate listicles purporting to describe *Extinction Events*!) One is called to broach in words that which cannot be broached because it always lies *beyond*.

Not for nothing—and here we patch through the connection in all its glory—does Ronell name that spectral telephonic summons that beckons writing a *call*. By her measurement, all writing is a haunted activity, full of ghosts in the wires who reroute and misdirect signals coming from who-knows-where:

> Writing is a depropriative act; it always comes from elsewhere. One is body-snatched, in a trance, haunted. Or, one is on assignment. I use that sense of being on assignment to emphasize how I am "called" to writing. I don't know how to locate its necessity. And one doesn't know where the imperative comes from. Nevertheless, one is assigned to it, so that one is always writing at the behest of the Other.[100]

By Ronell's measure, writers who attend to music are the paradigmatic schizophrenics. Delusional auditors of airwaves, they claim the music *tells them something*, speaks to them in ways in does not others, calls upon them to transmit a message on its behalf. Madness is this transcribing of telephonic messages from a (composer's) voice they do not hear, a voice that is, Brodsky is endlessly reminding, *the same as nothing*.[101] The illusory promise that one can ever know enough to say for certain how the ancillary and satellite fragments of textual material provided by the composer—titles, epigraphs, program notes, expressive citations—inhere in music is an acute form of psychosis, an impossible fidelity to an art whose very condition of possibility is the continuous deferral of precisely that inherence. Writers are forever, in Ronell's phrase, "responding to a call that was not made—but how, precisely, can we *know*?"[102]

It is difficult enough to write with—I do not say *about*—a music one can hear (to say nothing of *Extinction Events*' unhearable magic). Eduard Hanslick's old aphorism that "what in every art is still description is in music already metaphor"[103] stands as the eternal posted warning: music will do nothing if not put writing under extreme duress. *Lasciate ogni speranza*, because mere description of the object, what art history nobly calls *ekphrasis*, is not enough here. That has not been a lesson well-learned. Roland Barthes, scouring musicology for models on how to write the ineffable in music, stood aghast: "Are we condemned to the adjective?"[104] It's a conspicuous diagnostic from the one who taught that writing, true writing, is the space where identity gets lost.[105] *Ekphrasis* requires a stable author, some "I" holding fast enough to hear and to describe. A language of adjectives is thus, by his measure, an impoverished approximation of both music and writing, never sufficiently meeting the criteria for commensurate thought in either. (Barthes's recommendation was that we change the object under inquiry "to displace the fringe of contact between music and language."[106])

And yet—the maddening rejoinder—music demands discourse. The very naming of the object *music* presupposes a discursive capacity to talk about it, to index its attributes, its effects, its ontology. The instant we desire (we might say *feel called*) to talk of music, to identify *why* or *how* a music impresses upon us in some idiosyncratic way, or, more difficult, to theorize anything like meaning—there, at the very onset of speech itself, ideologic apparatuses have always already sprung into play, presupposing *how words mean music*. That these are frustratingly individual and sparingly articulate apparatuses, all varyingly self-conscious of their obliquity and contingency to the object in reference, is precisely why writing is demanded. To interpret music is to interpret its tactile interface with frameworks that exist only in the absolute present of the attempt to think it. Said another way: the difference between two musics is the difference in the respective pressures they wreak upon the apparatuses summoned and banished in the real-time activity of writing toward them. The entire project of musicology can be summarized as one long debate over the portability and rectitude of the apparatus.

In other words, all interpretation—from monographs to post-concert chatter—makes assumptions, most of them implicit, about what it means to traverse that "fringe of contact between music and language." More to the point, they make assumptions about how *music*, as an emissary of some anticipated meaning, midwifes or predisposes thought's compassing. This is perhaps what Nancy meant when he said that "listening is musical when it is music that listens to itself,"[107] implying that all human listening has always already failed to achieve a natural facility with the object. The task of serious writing is thus always voyeuristic to the auto-erotic touching of music by itself, forever forced to acknowledge its own desire for touch as secondary to this reflexive folding. A fidelitous writing with music would always already be telephonic, transcribing with no guarantee or security what it *imagines* (a fiction!) music's listening-to-itself to be.

Liza Lim is an acute case study in the consequences that arise when disparity opens between the auto-haptics of the music and its attendant discourse. If there is an unusual quantity of writing about her work, it is because she herself put out some very well-placed calls. An expert theorist of her own music, she has worked hard to scrub the static from most all of her telephonic signals, largely to success: her published analyses and explanatory notes form the bulwark of an unusually felicitous attendant discourse. She is a recursive thinker, both in music and in words, and her frequent retracing of familiar ground—shimmer, ecstatic transformation, fiction, ventriloquism, alchemy, ecology, hybrid knowledge systems, possession—has lent her attendees ample time to map it out. The success of that call is evidenced by a rare communal familiarity: New Music and its denizens can articulate her compositional philosophies with a lucidity few composers enjoy. Accordingly, the reception history of *Extinction Events* is remarkably uniform, not only in opinion but in fealty: most everyone rehashes the same few anecdotes and button-words she herself first offered back in 2018, as if a successful recital of *how she thinks about her music* were the same thing as *thinking at all*. (One gets the feeling that the parrotry has much to do with a desire for parental approval by the too-adoring writer.) Martin Heidegger provides the allegory of how discourses lose their rigor without sufficient disagreement in the form of the *rumor*. What often begins as profundity, he says, ends as platitude when it circulates only as *ekphrasis:*

> Perhaps the most thoughtful thought will today, and still more tomorrow, become suddenly no more than a platitude, and as platitude spread and circulate. This fashion of talking platitudes is at work in that endless profession of books describing the state of the world today. They describe what by its nature is indescribable, because it lends itself to being thought about only in a thinking that is a kind of appeal, *a call*.[108]

Lim's commentaries on *Extinction Events*—the treasure map of found objects, the eco-philosophy citations, the crystalline accounts of authorial intention—are profound only if they remain a switchboard and not, as they have been assumed to be, the call itself. If you can source the origin, if the call is not eternally *beyond*, if you set out writing *already with a thesis in mind*, it is no longer writing you are doing but rumor at best, advertising copy at worst. Composers are only sparingly reliable readers of their own work. Repeatedly describing their account as one's own supplants rigorous discourse with meaningless hearsay.

Extinction Events anticipates and redirects this habit—a habit that, like so many of modern music criticism's worst, bares the legible scar of capitalist influence—by leading the listener to a place where description is obligated to surrender. The final notes of the piece birth another of Lim's instrument-monster-hybrids: a contrabassoon, already impossibly low, is newly affixed with an extra 162 centimeters of PVC piping to extend its range down to the absolute basement of human perception. The work ends by crawling to the threshold of recognizable pitch and into the subsonic shudders of vibrational frequencies.[109] Notes become rhythm, a heavy "thud-thud-thud" (not dissimilar from Stockhausen!) that the human ear can only imagine as pitch (the quiet presence of a higher cello lends an aura of harmonicity, a trace that marks an absence). This is the ultimate shimmer, in which harmony itself appears as a kind of mysterious, ghostly aftereffect, a product of the hallucinating ear which still believes it can hear *something*. Three long calls, while the whispering cello hangs over and just beyond. Then silence.

We have been tracing the hallucinogenic virtuality of music's call to the writer of words. Here is that aporia spelled out: for how is one to *read*—critically, interpretively—a music one does not hear?

We could, of course, modulate it into the self-evident metaphoric apotheosis of the "Dawn Chorus": the song after the end of humanity will not necessarily be one we humans can hear, much less understand. This is Lim's reading, at least: "This music is not for 'us' but for a different audience,"[110] she suggests, paraphrasing her favorite phrase from Kafka: "oh, plenty of singing, an infinite amount of singing—but not for us."[111] It is the tidy answer, the answer that rolls with the tides. Or else we might think of the sick/health binary and recall the literal deployment of subsonic frequencies in vibroacoustic therapy: perhaps this is simply a music of healing, offered as the gestural taking-leave of a work that encourages us to acknowledge our *attunement* with the natural world. But these would still be only metaphors, and as such do nothing to absolve us of the standing obligation to take the moment seriously (the compulsion to be serious will, it turns out, be the entire concern). That would involve admitting that, properly speaking, *we cannot hear it*. We can indeed hear something, and we might even register it as pitch or something close. But the score notates and the instrument plays a determinate frequency (in practical terms, the F below the bottom of the traditional piano, vibrating at approximately 22 Hz[112]), one that can be measured and tuned with mechanical tools but cannot, definitionally, enter into consciousness as an object, precisely because its objecthood is the phantasmatic product of the ear's supplementary invention at the site of what it cannot perceive: we hear something that isn't there, or, better, *we hear that we can't hear*. We are all of us drugged hallucinators in the work's final moments. What, then, are the consequences a reading must assume—*qua* Kohn, a reading without recourse to the symbolic—when approaching a music that cannot be heard as itself?

Here, one last *mise en abyme*, the abyss at the end into which the ear of theory continuously falls back to the beginning, to the surface. It bears the name of "Dream"; the rest of the book will be about why.

A MONITION or A DREAM or A CALL

"Nevertheless, I must insist on putting up a sign here which reads: Watch out! Dreams!"[113]

The inaugural event—we might say the foundational structurating trauma—of modern eco-philosophy is Crutzen and Stoermer's nomination of the Anthropocene in 2000. The provision of a name, good speech act that it was, concretized an articulable entity behind which could be rallied the messy urgency of disciplinarity. Twenty-five years later, as evidence to its powers of centrifuge, orientation to the name's compass and the proposition of alternatives (Chthulucene, Capitalocene, Plantationocene, etc.) remain the dominant means of disciplinary identification for those who continue to work under its watch. Names are powerful things, and being given this one—this tractional, horrible one—was as traumatic as it was productive.

But that article contained a second, more diffuse speech act which, though no less foundational to the field's syntax of self, has remained more or less unacknowledged. From the vantage point of post-2016 eco-philosophy, Crutzen and Stoermer's article reads as surprisingly tame and nostalgically promissory, almost utopian in its stoic belief that there is time still to reverse course. But knitted through the article are turns of phrases, small omens of future calamity to which the paper would like to draw attention in the hopes of affecting their outcome. Here is one example, just lines before the end of the paper:

> Without major catastrophes like [...] continued plundering of Earth's resources by partially still primitive technology [...] mankind will remain a major geological force for many millennia, maybe millions of years, to come. To develop a world-wide accepted strategy leading to sustainability of ecosystems against human induced stresses will be one of the great future tasks of mankind.[114]

The phrase has none of the manifestoed hutzpah, none of the calls to action and panicked sounding of alarms, nor any of the immiserated nihilism of the reams of criticism that would follow it. And yet the second speech act, albeit in subtle form, is already there: the making contingent of a future of human flourishing upon a necessary, present action that will forestall a worse alternative is a very thinly veiled *warning*. Indeed, the very necessity of the first speech act, the naming, is in some sense only born out of this second more generalized act, and proves essential to the name's facilitation of the cognitive conditions for both making human ecological impact a *serious* issue and impelling the reader to mitigate that prophesied future danger. In other words, the unconscious form to which all eco-philosophy aspires—the speech act whose impelled hailing of alterity it desires at all times to engender—is a *monitory* one. Like Shakespeare's Casca in *Julius Ceaser*, who reads in birds and lions "portentous things / Unto the climate that they point upon,"[115] eco-philosophy is first and foremost a discipline of *warning*.

Which makes imminent sense: a grave danger is the field's unhappy object. But the place of monition in the psychic structure of the field has been undergoing extreme mutation. The originary warning has been sounded and unanswered just too many times, leaving the field with the realization that, in a technocratic too-late capitalism, warnings—even the high-visibility warnings mounted in public squares[v]—compel no sufficient corporate or governmental response. But

---

[v] For example: Olafur Eliasson's *Ice Watch* in London in 2018; the installation of the Climate Clock in Union Square in 2020; the annual alarms from the Intergovernmental Panel on Climate Change.

all warnings desire response; that is their fundamental drive. Hearing none, the monitory impulse—like all libidinal drives that fail to encounter their object—has had to make other arrangements.

In his chapter on monition in *Styles of Seriousness*, Connor attributes to warning a kind of work, one involved "in forming, formalizing, and maintaining *seriousness*, in the form of [a] precautionary attention."[116] The recipient of a warning is removed of free agency, because not-acting is now a choice: there is no claiming ignorance if you knew ahead of time. And so as much as warnings are performances porting significance and attention upon whatever it is they warn about, they are also incriminating imperatives: "well, you were warned!" But the ecological monitor [from Latin *monere*, to warn] does not have the privilege of resting on the usual promise of post-trouble rectitude (the future tense structure that, come what may, at least allows one to say "I told you so"). "The purpose of the prophecy," says Connor, "is always to allow the revelation, too late, that the prophecy should at the time have been heeded."[117] But there is no horizonal "then" from which eco-philosophy can safely launch its "I told you so." Species death precludes sober reflection on consequences, leaving one side of the warning's temporal container open and vulnerable. As a result, it has had to repress, or perhaps displace, the monitory impulse into other, more nebulous regions. For instance, one can read Anthropocene Studies' recent prioritization of less epistemic forms of theory—speculative fabulations, science fictions, affect theory, dreams—as a necessary modulation in response to monitory repression. All these entreaties upon individual consciousnesses amount to an inadvertent admission that the sole place in which a warning could feasibly be met by the seriousness and action it needs to fulfill its monitory circuit today has become imaginary.

Think back to the Kohn anecdote in "Admission." There, two Runa women are discussing what signs they should have noted earlier in the day that might have alerted them to the presence of the jaguar that killed the tribe's dogs. They debate the accurate interpretation of the spot-winged antbird call they heard while at the river. That particular birdcall is, in Runa culture, traditionally an augur [from *avis*, bird, and *garrire*, speech], a warning of jaguar proximity habituated by a history of symbolic human association. Connor, on traditional warnings, gives that structure: "The speech in which the [bird] conveys its meanings is ventriloquial, in that it is a speech projected into its putative utterer by its audient—it is, in a literal sense, hearsay, something heard as being said."[118] But Kohn rejects the reading that the women simply failed to heed the warning. Instead, he attends to Luisa, whose personal account refuses to circulate the birdcall in a symbolic economy, moving instead through a poetic modulation of sonic mimesis to arrive at an account with no literal meaning. Less urgent and more playful, perhaps, but Kohn reads profundity in her folding revelation: "Freed from the interpretive drive to stabilize the call's meaning," says Kohn, "Luisa was able to trace the bird's ecological embedding through a kind of play that is open to the possibilities inherent to the iconic propagation of sonic form."[119] Luisa does not start with the intention to answer "what the forest said" or "how the forest thinks" in human terms; rather, she lets sound guide her through "partial sonic isomorphisms" and homophonic resonances to end up with a poetic approximation that Kohn reads as likely closer to the forest's own reality.[120] This, he says, is good ecological thinking, "self-organizing thought which resonates with and thereby explores its environment."[121]

Already in 2013, we can see the modulation taking place. It would have been easier to say the women failed to heed a warning. Instead, the very structure of the warning goes psychically under, entering a kind of relay of mimesis and imaginary play that belongs wholly to the realm of the unconscious. Two pages later, Kohn will introduce Freud to bolster the credentials of such associative chains as undomesticated thoughts, suggesting that such dream-like associations are closer to how nature thinks, rather than man's Enlightened thinking *about* it. The implication, then—the implicit warning—is that we as a species need to get practiced at such undomesticated thought if we want to be ethically entangled on this earth. And if Kohn's reading strikes us as nobly posthuman, it is because we, too, have repressed the trauma of all those failed monitions. We're onto mitigation now, "rehearsals for precarity," as Lim says.[122] If mass warnings no longer have a central place, they are also not absent: instead, monition has been sedimented as the repressed desire, the hallucinatory dream of eco-philosophy.

Freud, for his part, is famously dismissive of the prophetic force of dreams. His concern remains with the past as a structure of the present, and in past and present's mutual participation in the single syntax of being. If there are warnings in Freud's readings, they come regarding the *practice* of dream interpretation, perhaps the most famous of which is his "express warning against over-estimating the importance of symbols in dream-interpretation, against restricting the work of translating dreams merely to translating symbols and against abandoning the technique of making use of the dreamer's associations."[123] The monitions Freud receives from dreams are against their own modulation into lexical symbolisms, as if the dream itself were warning "do not take what you think I mean as my meaning."[w] In place of symbolic warnings, Freud advocates for contingent, emergent readings, for meaning made not from the call itself but in an attempt to write toward the call's untraceability. The production of readings as the slow labor of a writing practice that takes no guarantees and assumes no origins: this is his real matter.

Freud's dismissal of the symbolic theory of dreams rests, then, on the necessary contingency of all interpretation. The unconscious does not toss up signposts as warnings of some future ill ("a raven in my dreams means someone will die soon," that sort of thing). If dreams do not portend, it is because Freud understands monition as a collapsing of the future within the past, which is at odds with his own thesis that dreams do not *speak of* anything. But Connor is slightly more generous in his reading of the prophetic structure, and in doing so draws monition closer to the becomings of the present—where warning shades into emergence rather than prediction. "Perhaps," he says, "although prophecy often seems to concern itself with catastrophe and apocalypse, the function of its temporal uncertainty [...] is ultimately *to keep history open, unconcluded, and revisable*, while also ensuring that past, present, and future remain looped together by anticipation and retrospection."[125] Warnings, in other words, are not predictions: they are contingent structures of attention and seriousness the interpretation of which (think of the endless narrative productivity from all those Greek

---

[w] He shares that warning with Kohn, and it's not for nothing that dreams become a central exercise in *pensée sauvage* for the latter.[124]

prophecies!) provides the foundation for action, an action which may or may not determine future outcomes but which routes the traces of both past and expected future back upon the present. Leo Bersani's figuration of the Freudian subject in time neatly draws the threads together and, in doing so, careens us back toward Liza Lim: "We spiral forward in time, which means that moving forward is indistinguishable from a relooping movement backward. Our futures are relooped, spiraling pasts."[126]

And what of a warning that is itself an unconscious dream? It's time, perhaps, to get loopy. You've been warned.

We are not going too far if we say that the apparatus of utterance in Lim's music, the very thing that compels it to articulate, is the form of monition. That apparatus is literalized early: in her first opera, *The Oresteia* (1993), the seer Cassandra is set loose on the performance space, an implicit proposal of the cursed unintelligibility of prophecy as a form isomorphic to Lim's own aesthetics of presence. Later one can see it submerged in her obsession with angels as "messengers from an invisible realm"[127] or the repeated presence of bird-human hybrids as augurs of distortion and extremity. Her notion of an invisible *there* which music, as an art of possession, brings into contact with our *here* implies that whatever force is on the other side *has something to say to us*: instruments and bodies become the telephonic routing system for portents from invisible worlds. (Not for nothing does Connor consistently route prophecy to practices of ventriloquy; Lim's predilection for the latter bespeaks the former.) Many of Connor's more abstract depictions of warning—"a complex stressory system in which the creation, sustaining, and melodic management of stress [N.B. exchange stress for *distortion, pressure, risk,* or *threat to stability*] are at least as important as defense against or diffusion of it,"[128] for instance—light up vibrantly in the arena of Liza Lim: warnings are not what it says, but *how* it says.

Accordingly, it is rare that her works make warnings *about.* That is, if there is a message of monition, it remains only sparingly articulable, even less nameable: warning is not *content.* It is form. Which is to say that warning impresses upon material, delimits and monitors its amplitudes. If her music is the temporary, controlled instantiation of threshold states of being, its aesthetic dimension occurs in controlled observation of the *force* ("Ah! What do I call 'force'? It is a matter of intensity, radiations, *the physical emissions of the dreaming soul,* of degrees of delight, almost always tragic"[129]) of their presence as it impresses on time and space. If it is able to do so, it is only because a monitory form is keeping that structure from collapsing or from damaging itself. (Recall Connor above: the creation and melodic management of distortion is equipoised by its diffusion and defense; both are necessary.) Lim's work pools serious attention on not just distorted sounds (sound as whole, as object) but on the very real limit-states of risk, possession, and invocation whose entanglement with Othered and Othering presence generates that granularity and shimmer. She asks us, in other words, to take those Othering forces *seriously* without relinquishing their status as Other. That she does so in this field at this late date in history is the product of a cautionary imperative she herself experiences but cannot place (Ronell would call this a *call*): her music is itself an injunction to reconceive how we index sonic ontologies, how we interface with dissonance and trouble. The tender attention she doles upon sound is propelled by a dread of what we will become if we do not. ("One does not keep one's dread in reserve; dread is this condition of virtuality."[130]) Monition, then, can be read as the imperative which compels her to write: rehearsing an entanglement with the forces that Other us in extremity as mimetic rehearsal for more ethical forms of species and interspecies relations.[x]

And here we come to that fundamental difficulty of *Extinction Events*, the one haunting this book without an answer. A composer does not write a work like this if she does not feel some imperative to *warn*. Lim's public activism betrays that she has this bone in her. And while New Music has always held at least one ear to the political ground, Lim was a major force behind the field's "Anthropocene Turn," unveiling the unique capacities of notated music to think generatively about what it is to be inside the age of meltdown. But the double bind of *Extinction Events*, like so much of the eco-philosophy on which it was nursed, is that this imperative is a repressed drive, a dream. *Extinction Events* withholds the alarum-bell, sinks it in the dark of night with the rest of the great ominous cathedral, and yet hymns from a place of worry. It suppresses its own empathetic urge to make a call to action. That does not mean the urge is lost.

Affectively, the "Dawn Chorus" carries none of monition's urgency. The contrary, actually: Lim has admitted the Waldteufels go on longer than feels right to simulate the patience necessary for listening to a music that is not for us.[131] But boredom is not without purpose, and neither is it

---

x Not for nothing does she frequently compare her work with erotics: extreme forms of sex share with Lim's music the paradox of a necessary active monitoring of the body in the thick of ecstatic loss, ensuring both safekeeping and the durability of pleasure.

merely, as Lim herself would have it, the symbolic experience of the necessary patience for listening to interspecies communication. On the contrary, no less than Heidegger will raise boredom to the status of a *call*, the answering to which involves the evacuation of the self that would make meaning of the answer:

> We *slip away* from ourselves in a certain manner. [...] In this casualness of leaving ourselves behind in abandoning ourselves to whatever there is going on, *an emptiness can form*. Becoming bored or being bored is determined by this emptiness forming itself in our apparently satisfied going along with whatever there is going on. [...] This emptiness is a being left behind of our proper self.[132]

Lim talks of "charging" the surface of the stages on which her music is played to facilitate the magic of possession.[133,y] In this vein, we might understand all of the ontological shimmer of *Extinction Events* as an extended rehearsal for the final, subsonic moment. We have, until now, seen shimmer in varying states of formal control: the found objects translated into the work, the folding plastic interruption, the singing of a drum. All these involve the skilled revelation of skilled concealment, compositional ingenuity that teaches us to hear both an actual result and magic spell. But the final notes of the piece contain no trick: their hallucination of shimmer is a real one. If in shimmer-as-trick we both hear reality *and* make it something other, in this shimmer-as-warning, we *do not hear reality* and as such hear something else. Practice and boredom

---

y The instructions for her second opera *Yuè Lìng Jié* (2000) ask that a Taoist priest be found to ritually bless the rehearsal space before staging begins.

have been twins, priming the mind to drop out at the crucial moment: here it is.

Warnings, we have already said, make it impossible to *not act.* They dispense—like Stenger's intrusive Gaia—with the option of not choosing: refusal to answer is already a choice. It is conspicuous, then, that the hallucinatory hearing that takes place in the subsonic ending of *Extinction Events* is compulsory: the body, *rising out of the unconscious*, acts of its own accord to create a ghostly harmony when the object sinks beyond its reach. What is compelled to act, however, is no logical, literate, meaning-making consciousness but the *animal imaginary that fills in the gaps where consciousness cannot go.* We make no effort to summon perception's harmonic mirage: it rises up seemingly all on its own—but not without invitation, and here we see why monition had to enter in as a dream. Like a monstrous ventriloquist act in which the direction of voice and agency remain secret, the repressed monitory desire of the music bypasses consciousness to call out to the listening unconscious, saying: consciousness will no longer protect you. That-which-knows is already ecocidal. The subsonic contrabassoon sends out its warning to *hallucinatory perception itself*, a warning that the body will have to act or lose. (Cixous: "It is possible to play on *m'agit*, who acts me, who inspires me, who makes me act, who prompts, who prompts the prompter [and on] *magie*," that is to say, on *magic.*[134]) It drugs consciousness, puts it under, perception asleep at the wheel; and for the briefest of moments—just a flash!—the infinitesimal gap of the magician who cannot help but blink as she performs the trick ("a split second of self-vanishing, where no one, not even the executor, can resist fading, disappearing, losing presence"[135]) opens—and the whole room hallucinates, bodies listening folding spinning where they cannot hear. When it's over, they will call it just a fiction. But something somewhere inaccessible heard the unutterable warning, remembers as it forgets: the body can still hallucinate, even at the limit of being. This, the secret desire which *Extinction Events*, saying, never says.

It is the feeling of secret we become acquainted with when we dream, that is what makes us both enjoy and at the same time fear dreaming. When you are possessed by a dream, when you are the inhabitant of a dream, you are driven by this, by a kind of heart beating: and the dream says something that is never said, that will never be said to anyone else and which you unknow; you possess the unknown secret.[136]

A Postscript or A Discussion or An Opening Again

In our techno-scientifico-militaro-diplomatic incompetence, we may consider ourselves, however, just as competent as others to deal with a phenomenon whose essential feature is that it is fabulously textual, *through and through. Nuclear weaponry depends, more than any weaponry in the past, it seems, upon structures of information and communication, of language, including on vocalizable language, of codes and graphic decoding. But the phenomenon is fabulously textual also to the extent that, for the moment, a nuclear war has not taken place. One can only talk and write about it. [. . .] It has no precedent. It has never occurred itself: it is a non-event. [. . .] The terrifying reality of nuclear conflict can only be the signified reference, never the real referent, present or past, of a discourse or a text, at least today. And that gives us to think the* today, *the presence of this present in and through this fabulous textuality. Better than ever and more than ever. [. . .] For the moment, today, one may say that a non-localizable nuclear war has not occurred; it has existence only by means of what is said of it and only where it is talked about. Some might call it a fable, then, a pure invention: in the sense in which it is said that a myth, image, fiction, utopia, rhetorical figure, or phantasm are invention. It may also be called a speculation, even a fabulous speculation. The breaking of the mirror could be, finally, through an act of language, the very occurrence of nuclear war. Who can swear that our unconscious is not expecting this? Dreaming of it? Desiring it?*

—Jacques Derrida, "No Apocalypse, Not Now"[1]

Ty Bouque:[a] We are no longer in Derrida's *today*. Ours is a different *today*, a different crisis. But there's astonishing familiarity here in the problems of thinking catastrophe. Steven, I wonder if you could historicize for us what it means to imagine at world's catastrophe.

Steven Connor: Several things occurred to me. I wrote some things about that essay when I was writing a book about the novel post-1945, when there was a genre of end-of-the-world novels.[2] And people stopped writing those! It's almost as though we survived nuclear war. Well, we didn't, but the thing about nuclear war that was absolutely plain to everybody—as it seems to me that it no longer is—is that it would be a matter of speed. That's to say, it was inconceivable that you could have a *bit* of a nuclear war. By comparison, I don't think anybody imagines things actually might go really fast in terms of climate breakdown and accelerating extinctions and degradation of the environment. That's what seems to make it if not completely, at least somewhat different from other imaginations at the end of the world. We're in more of a boiled frog scenario, and it's quite conceivable that we're talking about something that, at some point or other, will become irreversible. Or—*or*—we'll forget about it! Is that conceivable? I mean, I don't think anybody thought you could forget about the nuclear threat. But they went away. (Of course they didn't *really* go away: quite a lot of nuclear weapons were in Ukraine for a long time.) So the historicity of moments of the impending is

---

[a] The following conversation took place over video on December 16, 2025. The panel was convened to reflect on *Extinction Events* nearly ten years after its live premiere. The author served as moderator.

both very long and reassuringly familiar. But quite often there's a countdown—religious apocalypse typically depends upon particular dates—whereas we don't have a date with our particular destiny.

Liza Lim: That question of temporality is really at the center of it. But let me just skip back a little bit and say that climate collapse has already happened in many parts of the world. It's only that we're living in a very privileged situation that we can hold on to this idea that it's still coming. Thinking about the temporal frame in Australia, this is a colonial culture on top of civilizations of 65,000 years. So the modern, so-called Australia is a post-genocide state, meaning there are multiple temporal realities that sit side by side. That's why Australia offers for me really powerful ways of moving between temporal frames, deep time frames. Where we are right now is just a little blip, and if you change position in relation to time, you can imagine futurity in a different way as well. So rather than the last night or the last day, where I've gone with ecological thinking really derives and draws from learnings from Indigenous Australian cultural modes. Everything is relational: the basic unit of thought is a very multiple relationality. Rather than focusing on just this one particular moment or object, everything's always looping around. To speak technically now, there's this thing in my work about repetitions and incomplete repetitions, pockets of time and material that musicians sew into the other kinds of material. Likewise, I find languages that show different relations, different grammars of time really fascinating. That's where Indigenous languages are very rich: the Yolŋu, for instance, have this fourth tense of time in which you can say "we're gathered here speaking *as we've always been gathered* and *as we will continue to gather.*" Or, there's a beginning and a middle and a beginning, that sort of thing. That's what I'm really interested in doing with my work.

SC: That's really thought-provoking. You know, the anthropologist Robin Fox talked about what he calls *chronomyopia*.[3] That's to say we're really concerned with the historical period of human beings, namely, the last couple thousand years. But there have been creatures that qualify as human beings for probably more than 100,000 years, all of which is at work in us. And so I wonder whether it's a feature of our time, with climate change, that we have access to that.

LL: Tyson Yunkaporta, an Australian Indigenous philosopher of time, writes about this idea of deep time diligence,[4] that there are lineages of thought stretching back in an unbroken way, and song and ceremony holds that knowledge and allows it to be transmitted. Aboriginal people say, "Yeah, we've seen ice ages come and go, we've seen sea level rise." They have these extraordinary stories and songs that talk about the position of the stars very accurately 20,000 years ago. That experience puts you in a different position in relation to change. But what is absolutely urgent now is the change is happening so rapidly. There's no chance to adapt. We are the last of our species; we're in the terribly fragile place. That's the terrifying part.

Seth Brodsky: I don't want to get too programmatic about [*Extinction Events*], but for me, a light went off in thinking about the perversity of this music—and I don't mean that in a necessarily obvious way. But there is a polymorphous perversity about it. It's a music that is intensely interested in nature and in a way that seems a lot more responsible than other forms of musical nature-gawking. Certainly pastoral representation is not what it's about. But it's also very different than the Cageian imitation of nature according to her manner of operation. We've increasingly stepped back and realized that the kind of chance that [John] Cage was playing with was not so different from the chance seized by the speculator and the investment banker, the next stage of capitalism that was emerging alongside Cage. The fact that there's no natural coupling or automatic assembling or creating or forming or form in the music ... you hear a kind of openness in it, even at the end of the world. In some ways that's the most compelling form of openness to the future. The way I've tried to think about it is that even at the end of—and after the end of—the world, people will still be enjoying, coupling, doing, engaging in the fruits of what we generally call human culture. To me, one of the bigger things about whatever the human is, is this beautiful and terrible capacity to enjoy anything. Animals will adapt to a certain degree, to any habitat, and then die if it becomes too much. With humans, enjoyment is one of our ways of adapting.

SC: You're absolutely right. But it's ... *weird*. Benjamin talks somewhere about the dividend of pleasure that comes from contemplating our own annihilation.[5] As far as we can see, animals certainly have an apprehension of something that is *like* death. But we have a really clear apprehension *of* it. And it becomes the source of value in everything we do. A woman on the tube just this morning said, "We're here for a good time, not for a long time." And she's right: the sense of personal mortality as something that we share and circulate and amplify into the sense of a collective ending. And in one sense, if we were really absolutely guaranteed of immortality, personal or species, nothing would be worth anything. Immortality would be the only absolute evil, because everything would be empty of any purpose or value or beauty.

TB: Liza, could you speak on the subject of endings? What did it mean to end a piece like *Extinction Events*? What was how does one write an ending to such a thing?

LL: I'm going to be practical because I found my notebook! I was in Shanghai ... in the notebook it says "December19-20, 2017." So I was on the road when I wrote the last two movements. And when I'm actually writing, I'm immersed in the doing. It's the ritual of making and doing that carries me along. I'm not at all thinking of it in theoretical terms. It's an absolute kind of pleasure, pleasure of making and pleasure of contact, pleasure of welcoming. Writing music is visceral, somatic—and it's pure pleasure. I'm not feeling miserable and gloomy or anything like that. I was just very productive in these two days: that's what often happens at the end of a piece that I've spent months agonizing over. At the end, it just comes, because I've been inside this world so long it starts to make itself.

SC: And you knew it was the end?

LL: Yes, I suppose so. This sketch is exactly how it is in the score as well. And it's kind of simple, isn't it? I'm just sketching and making and rubbing things out ... it's just pen and paper.

TB: This makes an interesting point that I think ties us back to what Seth and Steve were saying about pleasure at the end. There's a sense, in the eco-critical imperative to *take the end of our world seriously*, that one has to knuckle down, quit having fun, quit enjoying yourself, get to work. But your music doesn't speak to that, and neither does writing an ending like this. It reframes what pleasure looks like, feels like. In some ways it rewrites pleasure as a tactile enmeshment with the world, a being-with-the-other that is both ethical and enduring.

LL: I may disappoint you—but I don't have a program around it, actually. Yes, it's called *Extinction Events and Dawn Chorus*, but it's not a didactic program to prove anything. It's very open-ended. The most important thing for me—which speaks to the pleasure—is binding and unbinding with the world. It's being with stuff: I like messiness, I like excess! The more stuff there is, the more I can play with it.

SC: There's a sentimental part of me that thinks that *muchness* is the human specialty or pathology, and that it probably comes from or is stimulated by the fact that we have this whole extra world that is formed by our capacity to model the world and represent it and convey it to each other, namely, language. So we have this representing apparatus which doubles the world. And now we have all kinds of additional apparatuses that double the world, meaning that we outpace and outdo it. In living memory—in my living memory, at least—you could still say that there were more things in the world than there were images of them. But that's absolutely not the case now. The world is buried up to the eyebrows in images.

SB: And we've just invented a technology that is capable of generating exponentially more images than we had the week before.

SC: Yeah, like *that's* the problem we want to solve. Also, not enough text! Not enough novels! Solve that problem straight away! Anyway. So I'm writing a book about exorbitance, and I thought I'd invented this word *auxetic*, which would mean augmenting—but actually Erasmus uses it when he's talking about copiousness in language, auxesis![6] So too-muchness is probably bound up with the fact that we're such talkative creatures, and bringing new worlds into being all the time. *And* we're also able to count, and we realize that you don't ever have to stop counting. Humans have a sort of exponential imagination which presses things to and beyond limits. And it gets us into trouble, because there are circumstances—as many cultures, most cultures perhaps, have known—where you need to curb these energies and ambitions and appetites. But they're very, very hard to curb. And one of the interesting things in thinking about the book was to look at the opposite of ambition, excess, and decadence, at the fact that we have an epidemic (a) of obesity, and (b) of anorexia. There's a kind of anorexic excess, which is a rather ancient and familiar thing: the ascetic excesses of early Christianity, for example, where it seems that there can be no limit to the things that you have the ambition to deprive yourself of. This seems to be alive and well too. And in a certain way, I do think that there is a purgative or piaculative fantasy—a fantasy here, not being a false thing, but something we want to be true—that we are monstrously and prodigiously and cosmically to blame. And like everything else, why do we think this? The answer is always the same: because we want to. We like it. We like thinking this. It's not very nice. It's not very pleasant, but we like unpleasant things. We are polymorphously perverse, and so I think we are in an era—but not a unique era, because I think almost any era that you would look at, if you looked at it curiously enough, you would find these energies of excess. So if there is a kind of excessiveness, it might be a passionate excessiveness of *dread* that human beings are wont to indulge.

SB: This clarifies something about Liza's work, and maybe in a larger sense about the role New Music plays in end times. We've come to enjoy representations, including representations of the end. We enjoy them compulsively and convulsively, in a strangely immortal way: there's an immortal drive to enjoy fantasies of one's own end that is completely distinct from and cut off from our biological organism …

SC: Well, that's because we're actually really hard to get rid of.

SB: Yeah, the evolutionary biologist would probably say only a pest—the human pest—could have this kind of apparatus connected to it. But so many of the forms of representation at work today are forms that try to shut down the amplitude and complexity and difficulty of representation and mediation. One of the really interesting things about *Extinction Events*—and I think it's a general quality of Liza's work—is that there's a lot of room to crisscross, to go back and forth between being immersed in the representations and being alongside them. It provides space to reflect on the represented activity, its representativity or representationalness. Now this is not a new quality of art we tend to call modern—in some sense it's constitutive. But it is striking how difficult fictions are for us today. So the idea of making the end of time or end-times into a fictional temporal universe and then giving it amplitude is certainly one place where I see New Music having something of a foothold.

TB: There's also another odd crosshatch with *Extinction Events*. Liza was talking earlier about these pockets of time, repeats that don't progress to find more things but double back instead to what they already know. But failing to make it all the way back or getting stuck in the middle, they get trapped in non-productive cycles of ascesis. We're just staying here. And yet in the spinning out, other secretions are produced, the spiral swelling of its own accord with slippages, mistakes, memories failing to recall. There's a paradoxical excess in ascetic repetition.

SB: That's really striking, because one thing we haven't mentioned yet is accumulation. Strictly speaking, the wisdom of the axioms Stephen was just offering comes from the fact that they are also admonitions against accumulation as the endpoint. "Be wary of the idea of gathering a lot in order to keep it, in order to hoard it, in order to max it out." We would never have been capable of destroying and extinguishing this world were it not for capitalism as a particular approach toward accumulation. It's really interesting to see contemporary forms of art making and representation across the board trying to inhabit the role of the surplus, contemptuous of their own status as representations. I'm with Anna Kornbluh here and the Immediacy thesis;[7] the question is where do we find forms of representation that are not geared toward accumulation? And what else would they be geared toward?

LL: In the book, you mentioned this Eduardo Kohn idea of "the self-organizing thought of the world": I think that, for me, is really the basis of ecological ethics. We just don't know so many things. Our knowledge, our positionality, is so partial. And so the distinction of thinking *with* versus thinking *about* becomes really important. I'm very against aboutism. Looping and spiraling become ways of thinking *with* time and living *with* time. That's, again, technical, but in this conversation, I keep coming back to the ritual technical aspect of making music rather than thinking too much about its meanings.

SC: I was thinking about this, Liza, and I was thinking about Samuel Beckett. He got into the habit of writing in French and then translating his own work back into English. And then sometimes he'd do it the other way 'round. And he must, at some point, have got into the habit of looking ahead to the job he would have of turning this thing into a completely different language when it didn't exist in the other one yet. And I wondered whether you might be, while writing music, anticipating, "God, how am I going to account for this?" And when occasionally people are nice enough to ask you what you meant when you wrote something, wanting to say: "you're on your own, really. I can tell you what it looks like to me, but it might as well be you reading it!" There are rather curious responsibilities of being *the one who's supposed to know*.

LL: Well, yes, I don't actually want to prioritize what I think anything is about. In a sort of fundamental way, the meaning lies with the receiver, with the respondent. And there's so many things I don't know. This idea that creators know what they're doing … they don't. There's so much that's really irretrievable in language too, so much unconscious. But that, I think, is quite a positive thing, because it opens up so much space for others.

Composer **Liza Lim**, AM, is Sculthorpe Chair of Australian Music at the Sydney Conservatorium of Music, an ARC Laureate Fellow, and winner of the 2025 Grawemeyer Prize for Composition. She writes music centered on collaboration and transcultural ideas. The roots of beauty, time effects in the Anthropocene, and the sensoria of ecological connection are ongoing concerns in her practice.

Cultural historian **Steven Connor**, FBA, is Director of Research of the Digital Futures Institute at King's College in London, as well as Professor of English Emeritus at the University of Cambridge. The author of more than twenty books on everything from language and literature to air and sports, his work haunts obsessively the oblique sites where cultural imagination overreaches its reality.

Musicologist **Seth Brodsky** is Associate Professor of Music and in the Humanities at the University of Chicago, where he also serves as Director of the Richard & Mary L. Gray Center for Arts & Inquiry. His work traverses the abyssal gaps left open by music's modernist unconscious.

Notes

Acknowledgments

1 Stanley Cavell, *Themes out of School: Effects and Causes* (University of Chicago Press, 1984), xii.

Introduction: On Believing Otherwise

1 Susan Sontag, *On Photography* (Farrar, Straus & Giroux, 1973), 64.

2 Liza Lim, "Program Note for Songs Found in Dream," last modified August 1, 2011. https://limprogrammenotes.wordpress.com/2011/08/01/songs-found-in-dream-2005/.

3 Karl Marx, *Capital*, trans. Paul Reitter, ed. Paul North and Paul Reitter (Princeton University Press, 2024), 1:19–24.

4 Liza Lim, "Liza Lim—How Forests Think," *YouTube*, September 17, 2017. https://www.youtube.com/watch?v=WN_2IU429Zc.

5 Carolyn Abbate, "Music—Drastic or Gnostic?" *Critical Inquiry* 30, no. 3 (Spring 2004): 505–36.

6 Peggy Kamuf, *Book of Addresses* (Stanford University Press, 2004), 139.

7 Fredric Jameson, "Cognitive Mapping," in *Marxism and the Interpretation of Culture*, ed. Cary Nelson and Lawrence Grossberg (Macmillan Education, 1988), 347.

8 Leonard Bernstein, "Tribute to John F. Kennedy," in *Findings: Fifty Years of Meditations on Music* (Anchor Books, 1993), 220.

9 Leo Bersani, *The Culture of Redemption* (Harvard University Press, 1990), 1–2.

10 Joseph Browning and Liza Lim, "Sonic Figurations for the Anthropocene: A Musical Bestiary in the Compositions of Liza Lim," *Journal of the Royal Musical Association* 148, no. 1 (2023): 11.

11 Browning and Lim, "Sonic Figurations," 14.

Admission

1 Dipesh Chakrabarty, "The Climate of History: Four Theses," *Critical Inquiry* 35, no. 2 (Winter 2009): 221–2.

2 Eduardo Kohn, *How Forests Think: Toward an Anthropology Beyond the Human* (University of California Press, 2013), 176, 177.

3 Félix Guattari, *The Three Ecologies*, trans. Ian Pindar and Paul Sutton (Bloomsbury, 2014), 18.

4 Donna Haraway, *Staying with the Trouble: Making Kin in the Chthulucene* (Duke University Press, 2016), 11.

5 Stanley Cavell, "Music Discomposed," in *Must We Mean What We Say?* (Cambridge University Press, 1969), 188.

6 Salman Rushdie, *Imaginary Homelands: Essays and Criticism, 1981–1991* (Penguin Books, 1992), 15.

Epigraphs

Félix Guattari, *The Three Ecologies*, trans. Ian Pindar and Paul Sutton (Bloomsbury, 2014), 37.

Jean-Paul Sartre, *The Emotions: Outline of a Theory*, trans. Bernard Frechtman (Philosophical Library, 1948), 58–9. My italics.

Martha Feldman, "Vocal Deliriums (Five Proposals)," *Critical Inquiry* 52, no. 1 (Autumn 2025): 2.

Extinction Events and Dawn Chorus

1 Friedrich Nietzsche, *Dawn: Thoughts on the Presumptions of Morality*, trans. Brittain Smith (Stanford University Press, 2011), 230.

2 See Max Horkheimer and Theodor W. Adorno, *The Dialectic of Enlightenment: Philosophical Fragments*, ed. Gunzelin Schmid Noerr, trans. Edmund Jephcott (Stanford University Press, 2002), esp. 1–25.

3 Lydia Goehr will cite the origins of her "work-concept" somewhat earlier, in the late nineteenth century. And while the concept itself is undoubtedly at play well before the 1920s, the installation of aesthetic taboos that characterized modernity puts pressure on the category of work in ways for which Romanticism can provide no precedent. See Lydia Goehr, *The Imaginary Museum of Musical Works: An Essay in the Philosophy of Music* (Oxford University Press, 1992), 113.

4 Helmut Lachenmann, quoted in Abigail Heathcote, "Sound Structures, Transformations, and Broken Magic: An Interview with Helmut Lachenmann," in *Contemporary Music: Theoretical and Philosophical Perspectives*, ed. Max Paddison and Irène Deliège (Routledge, 2010), 343.

5 Helmut Lachenmann, "The 'Beautiful' in Music Today," *Tempo* 135 (1980): 21.

6 Michael Taussig, "Viscerality, Faith, and Skepticism: Another Theory of Magic," *HAU: Journal of Ethnographic Theory* 6, no. 3 (2016): 460.

7 Michael Taussig, *The Mastery of Non-Mastery in the Age of Meltdown* (University of Chicago Press, 2020).

8 Lachenmann, "Broken Magic," 342.

9 Victor Turner, "Betwixt and Between: The Liminal Period in *Rites de Passage*," in *The Forest of Symbols: Aspects of Ndembu Ritual* (Cornell University Press, 1970), 105.

10 Donna Haraway, "Anthropocene, Capitalocene, Plantationocene, Chthulucene: Making Kin," *Environmental Humanities* 6, no. 1 (2015): 159–65.

11 Isabelle Stengers, *In Catastrophic Times: Resisting the Coming Barbarism*, trans. Andrew Goffey (Open Humanities Press, 2015), 43.

12 Stengers, *In Catastrophic Times*, 44.

13 Stengers, *In Catastrophic Times*, 47.

14 Taussig, *The Mastery of Non-Mastery*, 74.

15 Hartmut Rosa, *The Uncontrollability of the World*, trans. James C. Wagner (Polity Press, 2020), viii.

16 Anna Tsing et al. eds., *Arts of Living on a Damaged Planet* (University of Minnesota Press, 2017).

17 Esperanza Spalding, lyrics to "Endangered Species," by Wayne Shorter and Joseph Vitarelli, released March 2012, track 9 on *Radio Music Society*, Heads Up International, compact disc.

18 Taussig, "Viscerality, Faith, and Skepticism," 471. My italics.

19 Tim Rutherford-Johnson, "Patterns of Shimmer: Liza Lim's Compositional Ethnography," *Tempo* 65 (2011): 4.

20 Taussig, "Viscerality, Faith, and Skepticism," 478. My italics.

21 Mieke Bal, *Quoting Caravaggio: Contemporary Art, Preposterous History* (University of Chicago Press, 1999), 71.

22 Liza Lim, "How to Make a Woodblock Sing: Artistic Research as an Art of Attentiveness," in *Creative Research in Music: Informed Practice, Innovation and Transcendence*, ed. Anna Reid, Neal Peres Da Costa, and Jeanell Carrigan (Routledge, 2020), 119.

23 Timothy Morton, *Realist Magic: Objects, Ontology, Causality* (Open Humanities Press, 2013), 110.

24 See Morton, *Realist Magic*, esp. 110–23.

25 Taussig, "Viscerality, Faith, and Skepticism," 471.

26 See Donna Haraway, *The Companion Species Manifesto: Dogs, People, and Significant Otherness* (Prickly Paradigm Press, 2003).

27 Jonathan Flatley, *Affective Mapping: Melancholia and the Politics of Modernism* (Harvard University Press, 2008), 81.

28 Theodor W. Adorno, *Aesthetic Theory*, trans. and ed. Robert Hullot-Kentor (University of Minnesota Press, 1997), 79.

29 Lim, "How to Make a Woodblock Sing," 119.

30 Liza Lim, *Songs Found in Dream* (Ricordi, 2005), 45.

31 Liza Lim, "Rifts in Time. Distortion, Possession and Ventriloquism in My Operatic Works," in *Sounding Fragilities: An Anthology*, ed. Irene Lehmann and Pia Palme (Wolke Verlag, 2022), 203.

32 Karlheinz Stockhausen, "… How Time Passes …, " trans. Cornelius Cardew, *Die Reihe* 3 (1959): 10–40.

33 Lim, "Ecology of Time Traces," 552. My italics.

34 Lachenmann, "Broken Magic," 342.

35 Lim, "Ecology of Time Traces," 555.

36 Steven Connor, *Dumbstruck: A Cultural History of Ventriloquism* (Oxford University Press, 2000), 303. My italics.

37 Lim, "Ecology of Time Traces," 558.

38 Hélène Cixous, "What Is It o'clock? or The Door (We Never Enter)," trans. Catherine A.F. MacGillivray, in *Stigmata: Escaping Texts* (Routledge, 1998), 70–1.

39 Johann Wolfgang von Goethe, "Introduction to the Propyläen," in *The Harvard Classics*, ed. Charles W. Eliot (1909–1914), 39:251. My italics.

40 Emmanuel Levinas, *Totality and Infinity: An Essay in Exteriority* (Duquesne University Press, 1969), 50. My italics.

41 Avital Ronell, "Preface," in *Dictations: On Haunted Writing* (University of Nebraska Press, 1993), xii–xiii.

42 Levinas, *Totality and Infinity*, 51. My italics.

43 Sigmund Freud, "The Question of Lay Analysis," in *The Standard Edition of the Complete Psychological Works of Sigmund Freud*, trans. and ed. James Strachey (Vintage, 2001), 20:187.

44 David Joselit, *Infinite Regress: Marcel Duchamp 1910–1941* (MIT Press, 1998), 160.

45 Rey Chow, *Entanglements, or Transmedial Thinking about Capture* (Duke University Press, 2012), 47.

46 Chow, *Entanglements*, 55.

47 Chow, *Entanglements*, 46.

48 This figuration from John Paul Ricco, *The Logic of the Lure* (University of Chicago Press, 2002).

49 Deborah Bird Rose, "Shimmer: When All You Love Is Being Trashed," in *Arts of Living on a Damaged Planet*, ed. Anna Tsing et al. (University of Minnesota Press, 2017), G53.

50 Jack Whitten, *Notes from the Woodshed* (Hauser & Wirth, 2018), 143.

51 Whitten, *Notes from the Woodshed*, 296.

52 Whitten, *Notes from the Woodshed*, 74. My italics.

53 Connor, *Dumbstruck*, 298.

54 Lim, "Ecology of Time Traces," 548.

55 Jean-François Lyotard, *Postmodern Fables*, trans. Georges Van Den Abbeele (University of Minnesota Press, 1997), 166.

56 Lim, "Ecology of Time Traces," 552.

57 Lim, "Ecology of Time Traces," 552.

58 Steven Connor, *The Book of Skin* (Reaktion Books, 2004), 50–1.

59 Whitten, *Notes from the Woodshed*, 346.

60 Jean-Luc Nancy, *The Fragile Skin of the World*, trans. Cory Stockwell (Polity Press, 2021), 89–90.

61 Mieke Bal, *Endless Andness: The Politics of Abstraction According to Ann Veronica Janssens* (Bloomsbury Press, 2013), esp. 221–3.

62 Nancy, *The Fragile Skin of the World*, 90.

63 Hélène Cixous, "Author's Forward," in *Hyperdream*, trans. Beverly Bie Brahic (Polity Press, 2009), x.

64 Seth Brodsky, "An Infinite Amount of Hope," liner notes for Liza Lim, *Annunciation Triptych*, Emily Hindrichs, WDR Sinfonieorchester, cond. Cristian Măcelaru, Kairos 0022003KAI, 2022, CD, 9.

65 Brodsky, "An Infinite Amount," 9. My italics.

66 Ranjan Ghosh, *The Plastic Turn* (Cornell University Press, 2022).

67 Gilles Deleuze, *The Fold: Leibniz and the Baroque*, trans. Tom Conley (University of Minnesota Press, 1993), 34–6.

68 Deleuze, *The Fold*, 35.

69 Deleuze, *The Fold*, 36.

70 Deleuze, *The Fold*, 95.

71 Deleuze, *The Fold*, 5.

72 Bal, *Quoting Caravaggio*, 46.

73 Deleuze, *The Fold*, 94.

74 Deleuze, *The Fold*, 93.

75 Bal, *Quoting Caravaggio*, 36.

76 Hélène Cixous, *Dream I Tell You*, trans. Beverly Bie Brahic (Columbia University Press, 2006), 1.

77 Claude Lévi-Strauss, *Structural Anthropology*, trans. Claire Jacobsen and Brooke Grundfest Schoepf (Basic Books, 1963), 182.

78 Lévi-Strauss, *Structural Anthropology*, 181.

79 Lévi-Strauss, *Structural Anthropology*, 182.

80 Friedrich Nietzsche, *On the Genealogy of Morals*, trans. Walter Kaufmann (Vintage Books, 1967), 121.

81 See Paul Preciado, *Testo Junkie: Sex, Drugs, and Biopolitics in the Pharmacopornographic Era*, trans. Bruce Benderson (The Feminist Press, 2013).

82 See Avital Ronell, *Crack Wars: Literature Addiction Mania* (University of Illinois Press, 2004).

83 This figure adapted from the eponymous chapter in Carolyn Abbate, *Unsung Voices* (Princeton University Press, 1991), 30–60. On magical modernities, one thinks of Pietro Misuraca's characterization of Salvatore Sciarrino as "the Sicilian Alchemist," described as "increasing [the flute's] incantatory role and taking it back to its ancestral, magic essence." Pietro Misuraca, "Salvatore Sciarrino: The Sicilian Alchemist Composer," *Interdisciplinary Studies in Musicology* 12 (2012): 83.

84 Michael Taussig, *Shamanism, Colonialism, and the Wild Man: A Study in Terror and Healing* (University of Chicago Press, 1987), 461.

85 Friedrich Nietzsche, *The Case of Wagner*, trans. Walter Kaufmann (Vintage Books, 1967), 183–4, 166.

86 Timothy Morton, *Hyperobjects: Philosophy and Ecology after the End of the World* (University of Minnesota Press, 2013), esp. 99–133.

87 World Health Organization, "Climate Change and Health," October 12, 2023. https://www.who.int/news-room/fact-sheets/detail/climate-change-and-health.

88 Lévi-Strauss, *Structural Anthropology*, 180.

89 Taussig, "Viscerality, Faith, and Skepticism," 462.

90 Taussig, "Viscerality, Faith, and Skepticism," 464. My italics.

91 Taussig, *Shamanism*, 460.

92 Taussig, *Shamanism*, 461.

93 Taussig, *Shamanism*, 462. My italics.

94 Avital Ronell, "Queens of the Night," in *Finitude's Score: Essays for the End of the Millennium* (University of Nebraska Press, 1994), 57, 58, 59.

95 Ronell, "Queens of the Night," 58.

96 Virginia Woolf, *On Being Ill with Notes from Sick Rooms* (Paris Press, 2012), 21.

97 Stanley Cavell, "Music Dis-composed," in *Must We Mean What We Say?* (Cambridge University Press, 1976), 185.

98 Hélène Cixous, "A Kind of Magic," *Paragraph* 36, no. 2 (2013): 184.

99 Jean-Luc Nancy, *God, Justice, Love, Beauty: Four Little Dialogues*, trans. Sarah Clift (Fordham University Press, 2011), 104. My italics.

100 Avital Ronell, "Confessions of an Anacoluthon: Avital Ronell on Writing, Technology, Pedagogy, and Politics," interview with Diane Davis, *JAC: Journal of Composition Theory* 20, no. 2 (2000): 259–60.

101 Seth Brodsky, "There Is No Such Thing as the Composer's Voice," in *The Voice as Something More*, ed. Martha Feldman and Judith T. Zeitlin (University of Chicago Press, 2019), 227.

102 Avital Ronell, *Stupidity* (University of Illinois Press, 2002), 13.

103 Eduard Hanslick, *On the Musically Beautiful*, ed. and trans. Geoffrey Payment (Hackett, 1986), 30.

104 Roland Barthes, "The Grain of the Voice," in *Image Music Text*, trans. Stephen Heath (Hill and Wang, 1977), 180.

105 Roland Barthes, "The Death of the Author," in *Image Music Text*, 142.

106 Barthes, "The Grain of the Voice," 181.

107 Jean-Luc Nancy, *Listening*, trans. Charlotte Mandell (Fordham University Press, 2007), 67.

108 Martin Heidegger, *What Is Called Thinking?*, trans. J. Glenn Gray (Harper and Row, 1968), 49.

109 It is worth noting here that during the same gestational period of *Extinction Events*, the American composer Ash Fure was developing *The Force of Things*, a climate-inflected opera in which the "struggle to listen past the limits of our own bodies" is approached through a complex sequence subsonic tones that trace the opposite trajectory, gradually rising into audibility by the work's end. That opera premiered in 2017, just a few months before *Extinction Events*. See Ash Fure, *The Force of Things*, https://www.ashleyfure.com/fot-hop.

110 Lim, "An Ecology of Time Traces," 560.

111 The original word is "hope"; see the account given by Walter Benjamin, "Franz Kafka," in *Illuminations*, ed. Hannah Arendt, trans. Harry Zohn (Harcourt, Brace, & World, 1968), 116.

112 Which neatly bisects the range of 50 Hz to >4 kHz given by the marine biologists as the primary bandwidth of the Port Hedland fish choruses. See Milles J.G. Parsons et al., "Fish Choruses off Port Hedland, Western Australia," *Bioacoustics* 26, no. 2 (2017): 135–52.

113 Cixous, *Dream I Tell You*, 10. Original italics.

114 Paul Crutzen and Eugene Stoermer, "The 'Anthropocene,'" *IGBP Newsletter* 41 (2000): 18.

115 William Shakespeare, "Julius Caesar," in *Complete Works*, ed. Richard Proudfoot et al. (Bloomsbury Arden Shakespeare, 2011), 339.

116 Steven Connor, *Styles of Seriousness* (Stanford University Press, 2023), 180. My italics.

117 Connor, *Styles of Seriousness*, 195.

118 Connor, *Styles of Seriousness*, 191.

119 Kohn, *How Forests Think*, 175.

120 Kohn, *How Forests Think*, 178.

121 Kohn, *How Forests Think*, 177.

122 Lim, "Ecology of Time Traces," 561.

123 Sigmund Freud, *The Interpretation of Dreams*, trans. and ed. James Strachey (Basic Books, 2010), 372.

124 See Kohn, *How Forests Think*, esp. 188.

125 Connor, *Styles of Seriousness*, 195–6.

126 Leo Bersani, *Thoughts and Things* (University of Chicago Press, 2020), 69.

127 Liza Lim, email interview with Lucerne Festival, April 7, 2007. https://limprogrammenotes.wordpress.com/wp-content/uploads/2011/07/city-of-falling-angels-interview-lucerne.pdf.

128 Connor, *Styles of Seriousness*, 181.

129 Cixous, *Dream I Tell You*, 5. My italics.

130 Connor, *Styles of Seriousness*, 213.

131 Lim, "Ecology of Time Traces," 560.

132 Martin Heidegger, *The Fundamental Concepts of Metaphysics: World, Finitude, Solitude*, trans. William McNeill and Nicholas Walker (Indiana University Press, 2001), 119–20. Original italics.

133 Lim, "Rifts in Time," 201.

134 Cixous, "A Kind of Magic," 182.

135 Seth Brodsky, "One and the Other (Speculative Polskas for Karin)," *Portable Gray* 5, no. 1 (2022): 105.

136 Hélène Cixous, *Three Steps on the Latter of Writing*, trans. Sarah Cornell and Susan Sellers (Columbia University Press, 1993), 85.

A Postscript or A Discussion or An Opening Again

1 Jacques Derrida, "No Apocalypse, Not Now," in *Psyche: Invention of the Other*, ed. Peggy Kamuf and Elizabeth Rottenberg (Stanford University Press, 2007), 1:393–4.

2 See Steven Connor, *The English Novel in History, 1950–1995* (Routledge, 1995), 202.

3 Robin Fox, "Time Out of Mind: Anthropological Reflections on Temporality," *KronoScope* 1, no. 1 (2001): 129–37.

4 See Tyson Yunkaporta, *Sand Talk: How Indigenous Thinking Can Save the World* (Text Publishing Company, 2019).

5 "Mankind, which in Homer's time was an object of contemplation of the Olympian gods, now is one for itself. Its self-alienation has reached such a degree that it can experience its own destruction as an aesthetic pleasure of the first order." Walter Benjamin, "The Work of Art in the Age of Mechanical Reproduction," in *Illuminations: Essays and Reflections*, trans. Harry Zohn, ed. Hannah Arendt (Schocken, 2007), 242.

6 See Desiderius Erasmus, *On Copia of Words and Ideas*, trans. Donald King and H. David Rix (Marquette University Press, 1963), 35.

7 Anna Kornbluh, *Immediacy: Or, The Style of Too Late Capitalism* (Verso, 2024).

Index